PATHWAYS
TO
TRANSITION

The Art of Reinventing Yourself
in Today's Business World

PETER MCLAUGHLIN

Acknowledgments

I would like to express my heartfelt gratitude to all those who have contributed to the creation and completion of this book. Without their support, encouragement, and assistance, this endeavor would not have been possible. Their unwavering belief in me and my work has been a constant source of inspiration throughout this journey.

First and foremost, I extend my deepest appreciation to my family. Especially to my grandmother, Grace Ford McLaughlin, who helped raise me until I was 14 years old. A tough, principled, Irish woman who survived five wars including two world wars, I thank you so much. You provided me with a great foundation of hard work, perseverance, and a strong moral compass. You taught me to face adversity head-on and never give up.

To my father, John T. McLaughlin, M.D. A war hero, physician extraordinaire, inventor, and most importantly, a humanitarian. You were the smartest man I ever met. You were key in my reinvention process.

To Jim McElderry who entrusted me with a significant amount of responsibility when I was only 17 years old. Thank you for that trust, kindness and opportunity. You were my first great mentor.

To Tony Galinas, an executive at the old Grand Hotel near Disneyland, where I worked during college. You trusted me enough to make me Head of Room Service when I was only 19 years old. Which, still to this day, was a huge leap of faith.

To Bob Schneider, business executive, and entrepreneur. One of my great mentors who taught me just about everything I know about business and how to be a successful executive. Without his patience and guidance, I would not be where I am today.

To David Holder who wrote the very first check for Pyxis. He was a successful Entrepreneur, Venture Capitalist, Healthcare Executive, and mentor. You taught me so much about the venture world and creating companies. You also helped me create a large network.

To Dr. Jim Hamerly, former Dean of the College of Business at California State University, for the opportunity to work in academia again. Together we created the Executive in Residence Program and Business Professional Development class and curriculum.

To Mark James, my colleague and friend for all your tips on writing this book.

To all my students, both undergraduate and graduate who over the years encouraged me and prodded me to get this publication done. Particularly, Rachel Allen who never let up and helped push me across the finish line.

And finally, to my wife, Heidi, for your infinite patience and expertise in the field of writing. Thank you for your hours upon hours of reading and editing this book. You provided endless encouragement and support and you sacrificed much of your time to allow me to pursue my passion. Without you, this never would have happened.

Again, I am deeply appreciative of all the individuals who generously shared their time and expertise during interviews and discussions. Their valuable insights and experiences have enriched the content, added depth to the narrative, and played a role in bringing this book to fruition. Your contributions have left an indelible mark on this work, and I am forever grateful for your support.

-Peter McLaughlin

Table of Contents

Introduction

There are many books out there that are written to inspire success! But there are little to no books written about failure, adversity, or unemployment that can happen during the course of one's career. In an ever-changing business world, I was inspired to write this book after the employment devastation that followed the covid pandemic where millions of people lost their jobs, their businesses, and their livelihoods. People were forced to change their industry or their career path after years of hard work. Many had no idea how they were going to make ends meet.

Another reality in today's business world is the ever-evolving decision that many companies are turning to outsourcing to save money. Some companies have closed entire departments, leaving many former employees devastated, regardless of how well they had performed in their jobs. And it isn't going to get better anytime soon as the outsourcing market is expected to grow at a compound annual growth rate of 4% in the next five years.

According to the website Zippia, roughly 300,000 U.S. jobs are outsourced each year, and about 30 million jobs on average are vulnerable to outsourcing. High-paying industries that require advanced education and a refined skill set are among the top 10 industries that are getting outsourced overseas.

So where does that leave the average employee if this scenario were to play out in their life? What steps might you have to take to change careers and reinvent yourself to gain employment again? Thus the theme of this book.

What I have shared here is my personal journey. Writing about my own experience of job loss, dissolution of an entire industry, and going through the process of reinventing myself, will hopefully be useful to you if the scenario should ever arise in the course of your business career. My hope is that it will allow you to reflect on your own journey, process your emotions, and find answers to future success. Writing this book was also a surprising healing process that helped me look back at a sometimes tumultuous career path and helped me make sense of what happened to me and how I grew from it.

I'm hoping this book will serve as a source of inspiration and support for others who are facing similar challenges. Because it has now become a reality that people inevitably will go through job loss, career transitions, or periods of uncertainty during their working lifetime. By sharing my story I hope to provide valuable insights, practical advice, and encouragement to those who may feel frustrated and disheartened. Hopefully, people who read this book will find comfort in knowing that they are not alone in their struggles and there is light at the end of the tunnel.

By offering practical guidance and actionable steps for people looking to reinvent themselves after a job loss, I have offered practical strategies for identifying new opportunities, developing new skills, networking effectively, and staying resilient during difficult times. By sharing my experiences and lessons, I hope to contribute to a culture of resilience and self-discovery.

CHAPTER ONE
Nothing lasts forever

"Nothing endures but change."

— HERACLITUS

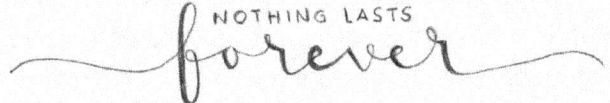

Knowing how to reinvent yourself after leaving a job or industry is increasingly crucial in today's business environment which is constantly changing and evolving. This is a result of technological breakthroughs, automation, and changing economic situations. While new industries develop, some may see a fall. The good news is you can adjust to these changes and continue to be relevant in the job market by being able to reinvent yourself.

Job losses and business interruptions can result from economic downturns and unforeseeable circumstances like the current COVID-19 outbreak. Being able to reinvent yourself gives you the flexibility to move into new opportunities and find work more rapidly.

Industries and work requirements are changing quickly as a result of technology. Certain tasks are being replaced by automation and artificial intelligence (AI), while new technologies are continually driving demand for new skills. You can stay employable and competitive by continually adapting your skills in response to these changes.

Careers are no longer linear since people are living longer and need to work for longer stretches of time. People frequently change occupations or follow various routes several times during their working lifetimes. Understanding how to reinvent yourself enables you to maintain a successful and rewarding profession over time and after losing a job, reinventing yourself offers a chance for personal development and self-discovery. It enables you to follow a job that is in line with your passions and values as well as to explore new interests and acquire new skills. Greater job satisfaction and overall contentment can result from this procedure.

Resilience and flexibility are necessary traits in today's uncertain business world if you want to stay relevant. Your capacity to face problems in the future and exploit changes is strengthened by learning how to recover from failures, accept change, and pick up new abilities.

Starting your own company or engaging in entrepreneurial pursuits are other ways to reinvent yourself giving you more influence over your professional fate as the gig economy and tools of starting businesses grow.

After earning my Bachelor's Degree in U.S. History but unable to find a job teaching, I decided to take a job working in the wholesale lumber industry in Southern California. At the time, California had the seventh-largest economy in the world. My focus was on the hardwood lumber industry, which catered to furniture, cabinet, and guitar manufacturers. One of my biggest customers was Fender Guitars. At the time, California was one of the largest furniture and cabinet manufacturing areas in the United States with over 8000 manufacturers. It was second only to North Carolina.

Life was exciting and my earning potential was growing rapidly. After working in the industry for seven years, I decided to start my own wholesale lumber company. It was definitely a risk but in order to get ahead, I took the chance. Eventually, I partnered with a large hardwood sawmill on the East Coast in exchange for millions of board feet of inventory. To accomplish this, I gave up 51% of my company. In hindsight, this was a huge mistake.

Here is the shortened version of the story.

One morning in June, after fighting the usual traffic woes associated with life in Southern California, I arrived early at my office like I always did, only to find my sawmill partner and his attorney sitting in my office. The cross-country visit was unannounced and a shock to me. My heart skipped a beat, I thought to myself, "This can't be good."

I quickly collected myself, and welcomed them both then asked "So gentlemen, why are you here, and why didn't you let me know you were coming?"

Getting straight to the point, my partner answered, "I'm exercising my option as a majority stockholder and taking over control of the company."

My heart skipped a beat as I tried to hide my shock. My mind started racing with questions. What was happening? The company had been doing very well. We were profitable, and after 3 years, we were doing ten million dollars in revenue. Why?

Incredulous, I said, "The company is doing great. Why are you doing this?" His response was direct and to the point. "Because I can," he responded.

My partner and I had always gotten along very well, and there was never any indication from him that he was dissatisfied with me. I was shocked! I had worked long and hard for years to achieve this level of success, and now it was being stolen from me. In hindsight, I made a Faustian deal with the devil by trusting him, and now the devil was collecting. His motive was pure greed, and it was apparent that he coveted the business and the lifestyle I had created in California.

I was married and the young father of three children, and now, suddenly, I was unemployed.

According to Psychology Today, wealth and status have always been symbols of power. Thus when you lose a job, you often feel a loss of power, especially by those who connect their job with their power in other areas, such as in the family and in social circles. Many people view their careers as a critical component of their self-worth and identity. Being fired, or in this case, losing my company, equated to a loss of my identity. This type of thinking fuels self-doubt about your worth not only in the job marketplace but also in the world in general. The loss of a job (and its accompanying income) also can lead to a strong sense of guilt—guilt over not being able to provide for family and loved ones or guilt for bringing stress and uncertainty into the lives of others. Finally, depression is a common reaction to job loss, and depression can lead to a host of other problems.

Although these feelings are normal, they can also be self-defeating in the sense that such negativity can have a dramatic impact on the ultimate outcome. Perceptions have a powerful impact on our thinking and behavior. Therefore, if perceptions remain negative, the likelihood of a positive outcome is significantly lessened. In contrast, if the negativity can be replaced with an optimistic outlook, such as, "When one door closes, another one opens," the chances for a positive outcome increase.

The Death of an Industry

In the mid-1980s, at an international trade show of furniture manufacturers in Los Angeles, California, I met Michael Shu, who owned three furniture manufacturing plants in Taiwan. Taiwan was becoming the next stop-off for manufacturing, following Mexico.

At that time, much of the furniture manufacturing had moved first to Mexico into what is called *Maquiladoras*. Maquiladoras were manufacturing plants in Mexico that imported and assembled duty-free components for export. The arrangement allowed plant owners to take advantage of low-cost labor and to pay duty only on the "value-added" – that is, on the value of the finished product minus the total cost of the components that had been imported to make it. The vast majority of maquiladoras were owned and operated by Mexican, Asian, British, and American companies.

Maquiladoras originated in Mexico in the 1960s with many of the plants located along the American border towns. (In Spanish, the word maquila means "processing fee.") The maquiladoras became a means of providing employment and significant foreign-exchange earnings for Mexico's developing economy; maquiladora employment increased from approximately 200,000 in the mid-1980s to more than 1,000,000 in the late 1990s. In time, other countries started taking advantage of this system.

In 1993 the United States, Mexico, and Canada adopted the North American Free Trade Agreement (NAFTA), which created the "Free Trade Zone" among the countries. This led to new American-owned assembly plants in Mexico and greater trade between the two countries. These maquiladoras made it possible for American companies to produce lower-priced goods because of the lower labor costs, but they reduced job opportunities for American workers. The latter was a hotly debated issue in the United States, and it contributed to a renegotiation of NAFTA in 2018 that resulted in a new trade accord, the United States–Mexico–Canada Agreement (USMCA).

I did my due diligence and traveled to Washington, D.C., to meet with the Department of Commerce and the State Department to determine the best way to do business in Taiwan. I struck up a friendship with the owner of the three factories in Taiwan and decided there was definitely a great market for a distributor like myself. The owner and I became very good friends.

By the time I started selling and shipping hardwood lumber into Taiwan, many in the furniture and cabinet manufacturing world were already shifting manufacturing facilities and jobs from Mexico to Taiwan. The logistics were a little complicated, but not impossible. As far as I know, I was the first wholesaler in the U.S. to start shipping American hardwood lumber to Taiwan.

On my first visit to Taiwan, I traveled the length of the island nation from Taipei to Kaohsiung City. I was surprised to see many of the large U.S. furniture manufacturers operating plants on the island. In conversations with my customers and various Taiwan officials, I learned that Taiwan was a mere stepping stone to China. Even

Taiwan knew that manufacturing would eventually be moving on to China within a few years.

During my trip to Taiwan, I realized that my industry in the United States was dying a slow death. I sensed that the furniture and cabinet industry would be gone within the next ten years. The United States could not compete with the cheap labor available in Taiwan and China. I was filled with a sense of doom, but I had no choice but to keep moving forward and hope for the best.

Today, 88% of all the wood furniture sold in the United States is manufactured in either China, Vietnam, Indonesia, or Malaysia. A small percentage is still manufactured in Mexico, and only 12% is manufactured domestically.

Later, while attending the Graziadio Business School at Pepperdine University to earn my MBA, I knew my industry was at a crossroads. I did my thesis on a Survival Strategy For the Hardwood Wholesale Lumber Company in the Southern California Market. My prognosis was grim. A very small market with very limited opportunity for growth. This, along with my experience in Taiwan, led me to believe that my industry was dying and it was time to make a change in my career.

Unlike many people who are forced into reinventing themselves, I did have options. I was armed with a BA and a Law Degree (JD). I had zero interest in practicing law, I just needed to figure out what I wanted to do next.

CHAPTER TWO

Coping with Job Loss and Unemployment Stress

"It's a recession when your neighbor loses his job, it's a depression when you lose yours"

— HARRY S. TRUMAN.

So how do you deal with the sense of loss and the stress that unemployment brings? While the stress of losing a job can seem overwhelming, there are a number of things you can do to take control of the situation. Make sure you maintain your spirits and find a renewed sense of purpose. Losing a job can also take a heavy toll on your mood, relationships, and overall mental and emotional health.

Our jobs are often more than just the way we make a living. They influence how we see ourselves, as well as the way others see us. Even if you didn't love your job, it likely provided you with a social outlet and gave structure, purpose, and meaning to your life. Suddenly finding yourself out of work can leave you feeling hurt, angry, or depressed. You might be questioning your identity, grieving all that you've lost, or feeling anxious about what the future holds.

Depending on the circumstances of your unemployment, you may feel betrayed by your employer. I certainly did. My partner was a man I trusted and had made very wealthy. There is a tendency to feel powerless over the direction of your life or blame yourself for some perceived shortcomings or mistakes. The stress and worry can feel overwhelming. But no matter how bleak things appear to be, there is always hope.

Here are some suggestions from *helpguide.org*.

Allow yourself to grieve.

Grief is a natural response to loss, and that includes the loss of a job. As well as the loss of income, being out of work also comes with other major losses, some of which are difficult to face. You may feel a loss of your professional identity, self-esteem, and self-confidence. You also may experience a loss of purposeful activity and your family's sense of security.

Face your feelings

While everyone grieves differently, there are healthy and unhealthy ways to mourn the loss of your job. It can be easy to turn to habits such as drinking and drugs. But these will only provide fleeting relief and in the long term, will make you feel even worse. Acknowledge your feelings and fight your negative thoughts, on the other hand, will help you deal with the loss and move on.

Give yourself time to adjust.

Grieving the loss of your job and adjusting to unemployment can take time. Go easy on yourself and don't attempt to bottle up your feelings. If you allow yourself to feel what you feel, even the most unpleasant, negative feelings eventually will pass.

Accept reality.

While it's important to acknowledge how difficult job loss and unemployment can be, it's equally important to avoid wallowing. Rather than dwelling on your job loss; the unfairness, how poorly it was handled, the ways you could have prevented it, or how much better life would be if it hadn't happened, you must accept the situation. The sooner you do so, the sooner you can get on with the next phase in your life.

Avoid beating yourself up.

This is probably the most important tip. It's easy to start criticizing or blaming yourself when you're unemployed. But it's important to avoid putting yourself down. You'll need your self-confidence to remain intact as you're looking for a new job or career.

Think of your job loss as a temporary setback.

Most successful people have experienced major setbacks in their careers. I know that I have. But, I was always able to turn things around by picking myself up, learning from the experience, and trying again. You can do the same.

Look for the silver lining. Over the course of my life, I have discovered that there is always a silver lining to setbacks. Look for the lesson in your loss. Ask yourself what you can learn from this experience. Maybe your unemployment has given you a chance to reflect on what you want out of life and rethink your career priorities. Perhaps it's made you stronger. If you look, you will always find something of value.

Develop new relationships after your job loss.

When we lose our jobs, many of us also lose the friendships and social networks that were built in the workplace. But it's never too late to expand your social network outside of work. It can be crucial in both helping you cope with the stress of job loss—as well as finding a new job.

Network for new employment.

The vast majority (approximately 85%) of job openings are never advertised; they're Filled by networking. Networking may sound intimidating or difficult, especially when it comes to finding a job, but it doesn't have to be, even if you're an introvert or you feel like you don't know many people. If you haven't done so, create a strong presence on *LinkedIn*. I will go into this in further detail later on.

Find a new way to define yourself.

For many of us, our work shapes our identities and defines who we are. After all, when you meet someone new, one of the first questions they ask is, "What do you do?" When we lose our jobs, we feel a loss of self. But it's important to remember that *being unemployed doesn't have to define who you are as a person.* It's up to you to define yourself.

Pursue activities that bring purpose and joy to your life.

By pursuing meaningful hobbies, activities, and relationships, you can reaffirm that it's these things that define you as an individual, not your employment status.

Try something new that enriches your spirit

Pick up a long-neglected hobby. If you've neglected outside activities in favor of work, now is the time to take a class, join a club, or learn something such as a foreign language or a new work-related skill. At a time when money may be tight, look for events and activities that are inexpensive to attend.

Spend time outside.

Work in your yard, take a scenic hike, walk your dog, or go fishing or camping. Spending time in nature is also a great stress reliever.

Volunteer.

Helping others or supporting a cause that's important to you is an excellent way to maintain a sense of meaning and purpose in your life. Volunteering can also provide career experience, social support, and networking opportunities.

Take care of yourself.

The stress of job loss and unemployment can take a toll on your well-being and leave you more vulnerable to mental health problems. This has been exacerbated by the Covid pandemic and subsequent quarantine. Now more than ever, it's important to take care of yourself. Treat each day like you are going to work. Get up, take a shower and get dressed.

Maintain a level of balance in your life. Don't let your job search consume you. Make time for fun, rest, and relaxation, whatever revitalizes you. Your job search will be more effective if you are mentally, emotionally, and physically at your best.

Stay positive and maintain your energy level.

Here are some tips that can help you stay focused and upbeat.

Maintain a regular daily routine. When you no longer have a job to report to every day, you can easily lose motivation. Treat your job search like a job, with a daily "start" and "end" time, with regular times for exercise and networking. Following a set schedule will help you be more efficient and productive.

Create a job search plan. Avoid getting overwhelmed by breaking big goals into small, manageable steps. Instead of trying to do everything at once, set priorities. If you're not having luck in your job search, take some time to rethink your goals.

List your positive attributes. Make a list of all the things you like about yourself, including skills, personality traits, accomplishments, and successes. Write down projects you're proud of, situations where you excelled, and skills you've developed. Revisit this list often to remind yourself of your strengths.

Focus on what you can control. Turn your attention to what you can control during your unemployment, such as learning new skills, writing a great cover letter and resume, and setting up meetings with your networking contacts.

CHAPTER THREE
The Early Years

Like many from my generation, I started working when I was very young. I got my first job when I was 14 years old. I was tall for my age and looked very mature.

Later on, a family friend who owned and operated a very exclusive private catering company asked me if I wanted to start working parties and weddings on the weekends. As an early mentor of mine Jim McElderry, the owner, placed an incredible amount of faith and trust in me at a very young age. He also gave me a lot of responsibility. By the time I was 17, I was running wedding receptions and parties and managing anywhere from 4-10 employees. Again, I was only 17 years old.

As a result, I gained valuable experience and people skills at a very young age. I learned decorum and responsibility, two skills that would become very invaluable to me in the future.

During summers, while going to high school and attending college, I worked in men's retail clothing, for a supermarket, a steel fabrication company, a construction company, a luxury hotel, and at a large steel mill. (The Kaiser Steel Mill in Fontana, CA.) All of this would help me tremendously in the future because of the wide range of jobs I held. I also had significant, develped managerial experience at a very young age.

Another advantage I had was that I wasn't afraid to get my hands dirty. Having Irish/German heritage and a Scottish grandmother who ingrained the understanding and value of hard work in me at a very young age, I was not afraid to do manual labor. Never have the mindset that a job is beneath you. Humility builds character.

In addition to working during the summers, I worked throughout college. I was an employee of Seattle University's athletic department. The institution was highly understanding of students who had jobs and attended classes. I frequently managed to squeeze some studying in between tasks.

When I made the decision to go to law school, I was also working full-time. I chose Western State University College of Law because I could go to school evenings after working throughout the day. A lot of really long days, weeks, and months resulted from this. It was incredibly demanding and labor-intensive. However, I felt it ultimately paid off.

CHAPTER FOUR

Reinventing Yourself or Choosing a New Career

People change occupations for a number of reasons and benefits. These justifications go beyond the possibility of a promotion or wage increase. People may decide to switch careers when the chance arises for a variety of reasons. They might take advantage of a new job that offers better chances for their professional development if they feel that there are few opportunities for promotion or personal improvement in their current line of work.

Career decisions frequently involve important financial factors. People may be persuaded to change careers if an opportunity arises that promises a greater wage or better financial incentives.

Often times it happens that someone develops a new interest or passion that fits with a different job path. When such a chance presents itself, people may be open to switching careers to pursue employment that is more satisfying and pleasurable.

Major life changes like starting a family, moving, or going through a change in priorities might cause people to rethink their professional choices. They might look for jobs that better suit their current situation.

When someone is dissatisfied or exhausted by their job, they may actively look for possibilities that provide better work-life balance, more job satisfaction, or a more positive workplace culture.

People might have grown current skills or picked up new ones, and they might want to use those skills in a different line of work that provides additional challenges or is more compatible with their expertise.

Changes in the employment market or technological improvements may open up new opportunities or make some professions obsolete. People may decide to change careers in order to remain relevant and adapt to these transformations.

It's crucial to remember that switching careers might present a number of difficulties, like learning new skills, getting used to a new work environment, or starting at a lower level. But when the perfect chance comes along, it can give people new insights, room for growth, and a chance to pursue more meaningful work.

A professional shift helps you to broaden your horizons and express your talents. This could lead to an increase in self-esteem and a better sense of purpose in their new employment. Though deciding what to do next may take some time, keep in mind that most career changers find contentment in the new industry they chose.

According to ApolloTechnical.com, over 39% of persons considering changing occupations are motivated by higher compensation, and only 14% of Americans believe their jobs are wonderful and they would not change anything. And about 70% of working-age adults are actively looking for work.

According to a recent survey, about half (52%) of American workers consider shifting jobs each year. 44% have already chosen to make a change. It can be difficult because not everyone has the means or access to do so. It can be difficult to consider your options without taking risks that may not work out well if you lack the necessary funds or time.

According to a Bureau of Labor Statistics Economic News Release, employees with pay and salaries have been with their current employer for an average of 4.6 years. However, one's age and career have an impact on longevity.

According to the Bureau of Labor Statistics, managers, professionals, and similar occupations had the longest median tenures (5.5 years). The median tenure for workers in service occupations was 3.2 years. Over the age of 65, the average length of only one job is 10.3 years. Employees aged 25 to 34 have a median tenure of (3.2 years).

What is the average age people change careers?

According to CNBC, a career change occurs at an average age of 39. After reaching mid-career, workers may experience emotions of stagnation that could indicate that their careers are going nowhere. As a result, many switch careers in quest of better employment opportunities.

CNBC goes on to say as people age, they change jobs less frequently. Between the ages of 18 and 24, people switch jobs 5.7 times on average. The typical number of employment changes between the ages of 25 and 34 is 2.4. Between the ages of 35 and 44, the average decreases to 2.9 jobs, and between the ages of 45 and 52, to 1.9 jobs.

How many jobs will the average person have in their lifetime?

According to Zippia.com, most people average working at 12 jobs during their lifetime. Thirty-two percent of individuals aged 25 to 44 considered a job change. And 29% of people have entirely changed fields since starting their first job after graduation.

Zippia goes on to say that one of the main reasons for these moves is a desire for a pay raise (39%), interest in a different sector (21%), and those seeking upward mobility (20%). According to the same survey, many Americans who went to school for a specific degree do not use that major at work. In fact, 21% use all of their education in their current employment, 53% use half or less of their degree, and 15% use none at all.

To summarize, the figures above illustrate that forging a new course is not always straightforward, and it might be tough to determine what you want to accomplish next. This decision is influenced by a number of factors. It can feel like an endless search until you find something that suits you.

Retraining can help in this situation. It provides you with opportunities and resources without the danger of investigating different fields on your own. With today's online learning systems and technology, changing one's job path is easier than ever.

Find the best fit

Starting a second job or reinventing yourself is not something to be taken lightly. Before you take the plunge, be sure it's a suitable fit for your talents, interests, and time constraints. Consider what you do in your spare time—do you have a pastime that could be turned into a business, or do you have other interests that could lead to a new career? "What would you do if money wasn't an issue?" is a question I frequently ask my students. A career shift will be most beneficial if it is for something that you are passionate about. Consider what inspires you and gives you meaning, and then look into potential employment in those areas. Consider your alternatives carefully and discuss them with friends and family.

Keep your expectations in check.

It's natural to anticipate things to be precisely the same as they were when reinventing yourself or starting a second profession. Conduct research on current developments and technologies in your present industry and other areas of interest. Recognize that there will most certainly be an adjustment period and time for you to learn about your new environment and organization. You may even have to start at the bottom and work your way up. Lowering your expectations will give you a better grasp of reality and will allow you to remain positive in the face of any roadblocks.

Whether you're reinventing yourself or starting something entirely new, chances are you'll need to refresh some of your abilities in order to prepare for your job change. You don't necessarily have to return to college or receive a new degree, but you can attend relevant classes at a community college, or trade school to learn about the programs and skills needed for your new work. If possible, take advantage of online classes to keep your abilities up to date. To be successful in a new career, you must demonstrate adaptability and bring an awareness of the new abilities required. Having expertise in industry-leading programs on your CV can help your job application stand out and provide you with the information you need to thrive in a new career.

CHAPTER FIVE

Reinventing Yourself in the Business World: A Path to Success

*"When Something bad happens, you have three choices.
You can let it define you, let it destroy you,
or you can let it strengthen you."*

— DR. SEUSS.

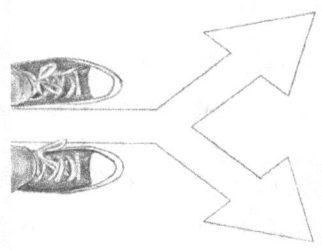

In today's rapidly evolving business landscape demands, one must be prepared to be adaptable and resilient to be successful. The ability to reinvent oneself is a crucial skill for individuals aspiring to thrive in the business world. Reinvention involves a deliberate process of self-reflection, skill enhancement, and adaptation to emerging trends and technologies. This chapter explores the importance of reinvention, outlines effective strategies for reinventing yourself, and emphasizes the benefits of embracing change in the pursuit of professional growth.

The Importance of Reinvention

The business world is no stranger to uncertainty and disruption. Technological advancements, changing consumer preferences, and global events can significantly impact industries. By reinventing yourself, you can proactively respond to such challenges, positioning yourself to capitalize on new opportunities and stay relevant in a rapidly changing market.

Reinventing yourself allows you to break free from the limitations of your current roles and explore new avenues for career advancement. By acquiring new skills, expanding your knowledge base, and seeking diverse experiences, you can enhance your value proposition, making yourself more attractive to employers and opening doors to exciting career prospects.

Strategies for Reinvention

Reinvention begins with introspection. By assessing your personal strengths, weaknesses, passions, and aspirations, you can identify areas for improvement and set clear goals for your reinvention journey. This self-reflection enables you to align your aspirations with the evolving demands of the business world, ensuring that your reinvention efforts are purposeful and strategic.

The key to successfully reinventing yourself is to make a commitment to lifelong learning. You should decide which talents are in high demand in your field and devote the necessary time and energy to learning them. Formal schooling, online classes, workshops, mentorship programs, or independent study are all viable options for achieving this. You can establish yourself as a competent and flexible authority in your industry by remaining one step ahead of the curve.

The digital revolution has transformed the business landscape, making technological literacy an essential skill for professionals. Embracing emerging technologies, such as artificial intelligence, blockchain, or data analytics, can unlock new opportunities and give individuals a competitive edge. By embracing digital transformation, you can reinvent your role, improve efficiency, and contribute to the growth of your organization.

Building a strong professional network is crucial for reinvention. Actively engaging with industry peers, attending conferences, joining professional associations, and seeking mentorship can provide valuable insights, foster collaboration, and open doors to new opportunities. Networking facilitates the exchange of ideas, exposes you to diverse perspectives, and enables you to tap into the collective knowledge and experiences of others.

Benefits of Reinvention

Reinventing yourself enhances resilience by enabling you to quickly adapt to changing circumstances. By continuously upgrading skills and knowledge, you become more versatile, agile, and better equipped to navigate unexpected challenges. This adaptability helps you remain valuable and employable, even in uncertain times.

Through reinvention, you can align your career with your true passions and values. By pursuing roles and opportunities that resonate with your interests, you can experience greater professional satisfaction and fulfillment. This renewed sense of purpose and enthusiasm fosters motivation, productivity, and a positive work-life balance.

Reinvention often leads to an expanded professional network, which can open doors to new collaborations, partnerships, and opportunities. A diverse network introduces you to fresh perspectives, innovative ideas, and potential mentors or sponsors who can support your growth. Expanding connections increases visibility and improves access to exciting career prospects.

Here are some additional tips on how to reinvent yourself taken from *positivepsychology.com*.

Establish a Checklist

Make sure you have everything you need to make the journey easy and doable before setting off on a mission to reinvent yourself professionally and emotionally. These things include:

Resilience

Obstacles and issues are certain to arise. Some of them will be challenging and might throw you off track, but what matters is that you learn from them, keep your concentration, and always get back up. To overcome these challenges, resilience must be built.

Support

People are social creatures. Having a support system that you can rely on can give you a lift when things become tough and correct you when you're veering off course. It's necessary to learn to rely on your support system when facing any difficulty. Finding the ideal ratio of independence vs. dependency is crucial. Don't be embarrassed to discuss the challenges you're having. You'll find the folks who are actually going to support you when you truly open up.

Self-Care

You will need to push yourself out of your old comfort zones, routines, roles, and self-perceptions as you learn how to reinvent yourself. This might be challenging and make you doubt your value, so practicing self-care is critical to keep your mind and body in good shape and retain a positive view. Exercise, spending time with your support network, engaging in an activity you enjoy, or taking the bus or train outside are all examples of self-care and meditation. Discover what works for you and what makes you feel most like you.

It May Not Be Easy, But It Will Be Worth It

Looking back, I know that reinventing myself was going to be an incredibly difficult task. I was leaving a brick-and-mortar industry where I provided goods and services for manufacturers and retailers. But as I said earlier, the wholesale lumber industry was dying, and I had no choice. Hundreds of sawmills were closing nationwide, and the 2 improvement centers, Home Depot and Lowe's had forced the closure of many of the smaller retail lumber companies and custom woodworking mills. The business as I knew it was evaporating before my eyes. That being the case, I learned a very valuable lesson. Never sit back and coast because nothing lasts forever. You always have to be prepared and remain resilient while watching for indications that change may be coming just around the corner.

CHAPTER SIX

Reinventing Yourself When You Are Middle-Aged and Unemployed

Losing a job at any age is challenging but can be particularly daunting when facing it during middle age. During this stage of life, it couldn't be more important than to be ready to reinvent yourself. People in their mid-years may face particular challenges that force them to change, pick up new abilities, and reinvent their professional identities. In order to successfully transfer careers, you must overcome the difficulties of reinventing yourself after losing a job during middle age.

Age Bias and Stereotypes

It's no secret that middle-aged people often face age bias, both conscious and unconscious, during job searches. Employers may harbor misconceptions about their ability to adapt to new technologies or assume that they lack the flexibility and energy of younger candidates. Overcoming these stereotypes and convincing employers of one's value and relevance can be an uphill battle.

But the job market continuously evolves, with changing skill requirements and emerging technologies. Middle-aged individuals who have been out of the job market for a significant period may find it challenging to catch up with the latest industry trends and demands. The need to update skills and relearn new technologies can be overwhelming and time-consuming.

Financial Pressures and Stability

Middle-aged individuals often have greater financial responsibilities, such as mortgages, supporting children, or planning for retirement. The loss of a job can significantly impact financial stability, making it difficult to invest time and resources into retraining or pursuing new opportunities. The fear of financial instability can be a significant barrier to embarking on a career reinvention journey.

Middle-aged individuals often face additional family obligations, such as caring for aging parents or supporting children through higher education. Navigating a career transition while managing these responsibilities can be overwhelming and requires careful planning, communication, and support from loved ones.

Confidence and Self-Identity

A job loss in middle age can disrupt one's sense of professional identity and self-worth. After dedicating years to a specific career path, individuals may struggle with a loss of purpose and a sense of disorientation. Reinventing oneself requires reevaluating skills, exploring new industries or roles, and rebuilding confidence in one's abilities.

Middle-aged individuals may fear starting from scratch and competing with younger professionals who may possess more updated skills or educational qualifications. The fear of being a novice in a new field can be discouraging, leading to self-doubt and hesitancy to embrace change.

Limited Support Networks

Middle-aged individuals who have spent a significant portion of their careers in a single industry or company may find that their professional networks have become limited or obsolete. The loss of a job may sever valuable connections, making it more challenging to access job opportunities or gather industry insights.

While mentorship is beneficial at any stage, middle-aged individuals may find it harder to find mentors who understand their unique circumstances and can provide guidance through a career transition. The absence of mentors who have successfully reinvented themselves in middle age can leave individuals feeling isolated and unsure of their next steps.

Strategies for Overcoming Challenges

To overcome the challenge of skill gaps, middle-aged individuals must commit to continuous learning. Seeking out educational programs, online courses, workshops, and industry certifications can help update skills and stay relevant in the job market.

Building and expanding professional networks is crucial during a career transition. Engaging with industry peers, attending networking events, and leveraging online platforms can help connect with like-minded individuals, potential mentors, and opportunities for collaboration.

Middle-aged individuals can leverage their wealth of experience and transferable skills when exploring new career paths. Identifying the core competencies that can be applied to different industries or roles can increase their attractiveness to potential employers.

Reinvention requires resilience and a positive mindset. Engaging in self-reflection, seeking support from loved ones, and developing strategies for managing stress and uncertainty can help individuals maintain confidence and persevere through challenges.

CHAPTER SEVEN

Highly Transferable Skills in the Business World

Some skills are highly transferable in the business world, regardless of the specific industry or job role. These skills are valued across different sectors and can contribute to success in various business environments. Let's explore these skills and look for ways for you to develop them and apply them to your individual sector.

Communication

Strong communication skills, both written and verbal, are essential in the business world. Effective communication enables you to articulate ideas clearly, collaborate with others, negotiate, and build relationships with clients, colleagues, and stakeholders.

Leadership

Leadership skills, such as the ability to motivate, inspire, and guide a team, are highly transferable. Leadership involves setting goals, making decisions, delegating tasks, and providing guidance to achieve desired outcomes. These skills are valuable in managerial roles or when leading projects or teams.

Problem-solving

The ability to analyze complex situations, identify problems, and develop effective solutions is crucial in any business setting. Problem-solving skills involve critical thinking, creativity, logical reasoning, and the capacity to make informed decisions under pressure.

Adaptability

Being adaptable and flexible in the face of change is highly valuable. The business world is dynamic, and the ability to adjust quickly to new circumstances, embrace innovation, and learn new skills is essential for success.

Time Management

Effective time management skills help you prioritize tasks, meet deadlines, and maintain productivity. Being able to organize your work, set realistic goals, and efficiently allocate resources is valuable in any business role.

Teamwork and Collaboration

Collaboration is crucial in the business world, as most projects involve working with others. Strong teamwork skills include the ability to communicate effectively, actively listen, contribute ideas, resolve conflicts, and work towards shared goals.

Analytical Skills

Analytical skills involve gathering and interpreting data, identifying patterns and trends, and making data-driven decisions. These skills are applicable in areas such as market research, financial analysis, and strategic planning.

Emotional Intelligence

Emotional intelligence encompasses skills like self-awareness, empathy, and the ability to manage and understand emotions, both in oneself and others. These skills contribute to effective leadership, communication, teamwork, and building relationships.

Project Management

Project management skills involve planning, organizing, and overseeing the successful completion of projects. These skills include setting objectives, managing resources, tracking progress, and ensuring timely delivery.

Business Acumen

Business acumen refers to a comprehensive understanding of the business environment, including industry trends, market dynamics, financial principles, and strategic thinking. This skill allows individuals to make informed decisions and contribute to the overall success of an organization.

These are just a few examples of transferable skills in the business world. Developing and highlighting these skills can enhance your marketability and open doors to various career opportunities.

In conclusion, reinventing yourself after losing a job can present unique challenges, including financial pressures, self-identity issues, and limited support networks. However, with determination, adaptability, and strategic planning, you can overcome these obstacles by embracing lifelong learning, leveraging transferable skills, cultivating resilience, and building supportive networks, you will be taking crucial steps toward successful career transitions. By embracing change and remaining open to new opportunities, you can embark on a journey of reinvention, discovering fulfilling and rewarding paths that align with your aspirations and talents.

CHAPTER EIGHT
My Personal Journey Through the Reinvention Process

The 1984 Summer Olympics.
"The most important thing in the Olympic Games is not winning but taking part; the essential thing in life is not conquering but fighting well."

— *PIERRE DE COUBERTIN*
(PRIMARILY RESPONSIBLE FOR THE REVIVAL OF THE OLYMPIC GAMES IN 1894)

In 1983 I had the good fortune to meet David L. Wolper who was a successful television and film producer, responsible for shows such as *Roots*, *The Thorn Birds*, and *North and South*, and the theatrically-released films *L.A. Confidential* and *Willy Wonka & the Chocolate Factory*. A childhood friend of mine worked for him and invited me to have lunch with her and David over at the Warner Bros. Studios in Burbank, California.

At the time, I was aware that David was very much responsible for bringing the upcoming 1984 Summer Olympics to Los Angeles. David's professional introduction to the Olympic world took place when the Munich Olympic Organizing Committee chose him to produce the official film of the 1972 Olympic Games. "Visions of Eight" was produced using his concept of documenting the Munich Olympics through the camera lenses of eight noted international directors.

A few years later, David became active in the bid to bring the 1984 Olympic Games to Los Angeles, eventually being named by Mayor Tom Bradley to the "Committee of Seven," a group of civic leaders who secured the Games for Los Angeles through a series of successful negotiations with the International Olympic Committee. David later became Vice-Chairman of the Los Angeles Olympic Organizing Committee, a member of the Executive Committee of the Board of Directors, and Chairman of the LAOOC's Television Commission.

A year before the Los Angeles Games, Mr. Wolper accepted the position of Commissioner of Ceremonies. His subsequent production of the critically acclaimed Opening and Closing Ceremonies for the 1984 Olympic Games helped to make him one of the best-known producers in the world.

Over lunch, the conversation naturally drifted toward the upcoming Olympics. David asked me if I would be interested in working with him and the planning committee for the Games. I told him I would love the opportunity. After our lunch, he made some phone introductions, and I found myself working with a group of volunteers at an office in Westwood, California. For the next year, a large group of us were responsible for interviewing approximately 45,000 would-be volunteers who would work at various venues for the Summer Games.

I am very proud to say it was ultimately one of the greatest experiences of my life. The lessons I learned and the experience of helping put together one of the most successful Olympics ever (based on return on investment - ROI), was one of the milestones of my career. The business lessons learned were invaluable. I learned a lot from both Peter Ueberroth and Harry Usher while helping produce an Olympics that netted $220 million dollars.

In hindsight, this helped prepare me for the drastic change and transition that was approaching in my life. Experience is always the best teacher, and in this case, it was. I learned both hard and soft skills that are still valuable to me today. Also, the experience taught me how to think on my feet and to be prepared for just about anything, including extemporaneous speaking.

One of the training sites was a synchronized swimming facility located in Cerritos, California. I received a request to discuss the impending Olympic events at a Cerritos City Council meeting just before the events began. As opposed to what I had anticipated, I ended up speaking to about 200 individuals. and it was undoubtedly one of the most uncomfortable situations in my professional experience, but I pulled it off. It made me realize how important it was to be able to think on my feet and communicate quickly.

CHAPTER NINE
PYXIS

Human subtlety will never devise an invention more beautiful, more simple or more direct than does nature because in her inventions nothing is lacking, and nothing is superfluous.

— LEONARDO DA VINCI

My father was a well-respected physician at Glendale Memorial Hospital in Glendale, California. He was a surgeon and an oncologist, and Chair of the Pharmacy Committee at the hospital. Over the years, he had learned some unsettling news about the way patients were medicated.

He was appalled at the number of medication errors in hospitals nationwide. So my dad, a lifelong inventor, set out to solve the problem.

My father was an army flight surgeon during World War II. During the war, he invented an oxygen-monitoring system for high-flying bombers. The system would calculate return trips for the planes in case their oxygen tanks were ruptured by enemy fire, telling pilots how long and at what altitude they could fly to make it home safely.

So in 1980, he had the idea to develop a dispensing device that would assist in reducing prescription errors in hospitals. He imagined an automated system that would avoid medicine dispensing mistakes and relieve medical staff of time-consuming paperwork. It also would lessen theft, which was also a big problem in the medical field.

The system would require a password to enter, would keep records of medication dispensed to patients, and would alert the pharmacy when supplies would run low.

As chairman of the hospital's pharmacy committee, he learned that there was an average of one drug error per day per patient in any given hospital all over the country, according to a study published in the New England Journal of Medicine. Human error was inevitable when the average patient was getting more than six medications a day, it was thus necessitating an automated system that guarded against those errors.

He enlisted the help of my brother, who had a background in physics and electronics, my sister, who was a licensed Psychologist, and myself with a business background and the experience of starting my own company.

Originally, his idea was to place a small device in every patient's room which would sound an alarm to remind the patient to take their medication. It would also emit an alarm at the nursing station to remind the nurses to dispense the medication to the patient.

The original prototypes were built out of simple plywood and some off-the-shelf electronics. My brother did all of the hand assembly on the prototypes. We spent our spare time in the garage and on the weekends tinkering and tweaking this new device.

After several years and raising a small amount of angel capital, we had a number of prototypes built and beta-tested at the Long Beach Veterans Hospital. The administrators there loved the product, and the tests were successful. This led to some additional testing at Baylor University, and after that testing session, we received some positive reviews from some respected journals in the healthcare industry.

This gave us the momentum we needed to move forward and raise some additional capital. In this case, we were able to raise venture capital with a firm in San Diego named Biovest Partners. Tim Wollaeger and Ted Green were the founders. With the hiring of Ron Taylor as the CEO, the company took off.

We had informally called our company McLaughlin Electronics, but Tim Wollaeger came up with the idea to name the company Pyxis. A pyxis is the shape of a vessel from the classical world, usually a cylindrical box with a separate lid. Originally mostly used by women to hold cosmetics, trinkets, or jewelry.

By 1990, almost every hospital in the country was using our medication dispensing system and after several rounds of funding, one being a down round, Pyxis went public on the New York Stock Exchange in July of 1992. With the money we made from the Initial

Public Offering (IPO) and subsequent stock, we were able to continue working on other inventions and technologies and operate as consultants in the medical technology industry.

In 1996 Pyxis was acquired by Cardinal Healthcare for $867 million. In 2009 Pyxis was spun off as an independent medical technology company renamed CareFusion. In 2014, Becton Dickinson acquired the company for $12.2 billion.

It's amazing that this was the result of one idea and a lot of effort from a group of "non-techy" people who built the first prototype in my father's garage.

CHAPTER TEN
Job Security Is a Big Lie

No one really has any job security anymore, including myself.

— SIMON COWELL

Job security has long been regarded as a pillar of stability in the business world, providing employees with a sense of financial certainty and peace of mind. However, the changing dynamics of the modern business environment have raised questions about the existence of traditional notions of job security. This chapter will explore the multifaceted nature of job security in the business world today, considering factors such as technological advancements, globalization, economic fluctuations, and evolving workforce dynamics.

One of the significant shifts in the modern business world is the changing dynamics of the workforce. Gone are the days of lifelong employment and predictable career paths. The current workforce embraces greater mobility and flexibility, seeking diverse experiences and opportunities for personal growth. While this may suggest a decline in traditional job security, it also presents new avenues for career development, you can enhance your job security by actively adapting to changing job market demands, investing in continuous learning, and acquiring new skills that are in high demand.

The existence of job security can vary significantly across industries and individual companies. Certain sectors, such as healthcare, education, government, and essential services, often provide more stable employment due to the persistent demand for their services. Established companies with a strong market presence and a focus on employee well-being and retention also tend to prioritize job security as part of their organizational culture. By aligning yourself with these types of stable industries or reputable companies, you can enhance your prospects of job security.

Technological Advances

Technological advancements have revolutionized the business landscape, bringing about both opportunities and challenges.

Automation, artificial intelligence, and robotics have led to the displacement of certain jobs, causing concerns about job security. However, it is important to note that these technological developments also create new job roles and industries. Job security in this context becomes closely tied to your ability to adapt to technological changes, acquire new skills, and remain relevant in an ever-evolving job market. Lifelong learning and upskilling become crucial for maintaining job security in the face of technological disruptions.

Economic and Market Conditions

Job security is significantly influenced by economic and market conditions. Economic fluctuations and market disruptions can lead to downsizing, restructuring, and layoffs as companies aim to cut costs. During such periods, job security may become more precarious. However, in times of economic growth and expansion, businesses tend to hire more employees and provide greater job security. Therefore, macroeconomic stability plays a critical role in determining the level of job security available in the business world.

Entrepreneurship and Gig Economy

The term "gig economy" refers to a labor market characterized by the prevalence of short-term or freelance work arrangements, where individuals often work on a project basis or perform tasks on a temporary basis. Usually, the work is performed as an independent contractor. In the gig economy, instead of having traditional long-term employment with a single employer, workers engage in a series of temporary jobs, contracts, or freelance work, typically facilitated through digital platforms or online marketplaces.

The gig economy has been facilitated by advances in technology and the proliferation of online platforms that connect gig workers with individuals or businesses in need of their services. It has provided opportunities for individuals to earn income outside of traditional employment structures, but it has also raised concerns about worker rights, job security, benefits, and the potential for exploitation due to the lack of formal employment protections in many cases.

The rise of entrepreneurship and the gig economy has redefined the traditional employment landscape. While these alternative forms of work offer flexibility and autonomy, they may not provide the same level of job security as traditional employment. Individuals in these roles must actively manage their income streams, cultivate a diverse client base, and adapt to market changes to maintain financial stability. While the gig economy offers opportunities, it may also bring uncertainties and fluctuations in income.

In conclusion, job security in the business world today is a complex and evolving concept. Traditional notions of lifelong employment and guaranteed job security have undergone significant transformations. The changing workforce dynamics, technological advancements, economic conditions, and the rise of alternative work arrangements have reshaped the landscape of job security. While the concept of job security may not be as straightforward as it once was, you can enhance your prospects by embracing lifelong learning, staying adaptable, and acquiring versatile skill sets that align with the changing demands of the job market. The key lies in recognizing the evolving nature of job security and proactively navigating the opportunities and challenges presented by the modern business world.

CHAPTER ELEVEN
Is a College Degree Always Necessary for Today's Job Market?

Training is everything. The peach was once a bitter almond; cauliflower is nothing but cabbage with a college education.

— MARK TWAIN

As the U.S. labor market continues to recover from the effects of the COVID-19 pandemic, one constant remains: Education boosts earnings and reduces unemployment. Let's take an honest look into the reality of obtaining a college degree and the pros and cons involved in making your decision.

The chart below highlights differences in 2021 earnings and unemployment rates by educational attainment, using data from the U.S. Bureau of Labor Statistics (BLS) Current Population Survey (CPS). Workers aged 25 and over who attained less than a high school diploma had the lowest median weekly earnings ($626) and highest unemployment rate (8.3 percent) among those at all education levels. Workers with graduate degrees (master's, professional, and doctoral degrees) had the highest earnings and lowest unemployment rates.

From the U.S. Bureau of Labor Statistics

Earnings and unemployment rates by educational attainment, 2021

Educational attainment	Median usual weekly earnings	Unemployment rate
Doctoral degree	$1,909	1.5%
Professional degree	1,924	1.8
Master's degree	1,574	2.6
Bachelor's degree	1,334	3.5
Associate's degree	963	4.6
Some college, no degree	899	5.5
High school diploma	809	6.2
Less than a high school diploma	626	8.3

Note: Data are for persons age 25 and over. Earnings are for full-time wage and salary workers.
Source: U.S. Bureau of Labor Statistics, Current Population Survey.

Teachers, guidance counselors, and other well-intentioned people have probably repeatedly informed young kids that they must go to college to make a successful living over the years. But is a college degree always worthwhile in the employment environment of today?

Since I was in school, college has become significantly more expensive. Costs have climbed by nearly 25% in the last ten years, and the majority of college graduates graduate with sizable debts from student loans. A bachelor's degree can still be beneficial in the long term, though, but here are some things to think about while determining whether or not college is right for you.

Be ready for sticker shock if you intend to attend college. The average total cost of attendance at a public university for in-state students is $27,330 per year, according to the College Board's report from 2021, whereas the average total cost of attendance at private colleges is $55,800 per year. Depending on the type of institution you attend, your degree would cost between $109,320 and $223,200 if you were to graduate in four years.

Even if you are eligible for financial aid like scholarships and grants, that cost can still be prohibitive. Make sure to ask yourself, "Is college worth it for me and my career goals?" before making the decision to enroll.

Financial Considerations and Return on Investment

Concerns regarding the financial worth of earning a college degree have been raised in light of the escalating cost of tuition. The prospective return on investment (ROI) in terms of future revenue and professional development must be carefully considered. While it is true that not all college degrees lead to well-paying careers, statistical evidence repeatedly shows that those with college degrees often have better lifetime earnings than those without. To lessen the financial load, it is crucial to take into account aspects like student loan debt, scholarship prospects, and prospective financial aid.

Evolving Job Market Dynamics

Recognizing the changing dynamics of the labor market is crucial. There has been an increase in the need for specialized training and occupational skills in recent years. Some contend that the conventional college degree may not address these increasing skill gaps. Businesses in fields like technology, data science, and skilled professions frequently place more value on specialized certificates or job-specific training than on generic degrees. To guarantee that their educational choices and professional ambitions are in line, people thinking about getting a college degree should carefully assess the current market trends and industry needs.

Knowledge Acquisition and Intellectual Development

Learning new things and expanding one's mind are essential components of earning a college degree. Students who attend - college benefit from an organized learning environment where they can complete challenging coursework, conduct research, and exercise critical thinking. A well-rounded education is fostered through exposure to a variety of academic fields, which improves one's capacity for communication, analytical thought, and problem-solving. These abilities are widely sought after in the job market because they allow graduates to successfully adjust to shifting work situations.

Job Market Demand and Employability

Even though the employment market is continually changing, applicants with college degrees are still valued and given preference in numerous areas. Certain occupations, including those in health, law, engineering, and academics, call for advanced degrees and specialized training. Additionally, a college degree is frequently used by companies as a screening criterion to evaluate a candidate's commitment, discipline, and aptitude for learning. It serves as a starting point that distinguishes applicants from those without a degree, improving their chances of finding employment.

Career Opportunities and Advancement

A college degree can set the route for professional advancement and provide access to a larger range of work prospects. Numerous lucrative jobs with high salaries have educational prerequisites, including a college degree. Graduates frequently have an easier time finding entry-level jobs in their chosen fields, and as they gain experience, their chances of getting promoted may improve. Further specialization or advanced degrees can be built on a degree, allowing people to pursue more specialized career paths and senior-level roles.

Networking and Access to Resources

Universities and colleges provide graduates with beneficial networking opportunities that can help them throughout their careers. Campus settings encourage relationships with classmates, instructors, and business leaders, opening doors to internship opportunities, mentorship programs, and job placement services. These networks offer a venue for teamwork, information exchange, and potential job introductions. Additionally, educational institutions frequently give students access to sizable libraries, research centers, and other tools that assist continued education and career advancement.

Entrepreneurship and Innovation

A college education can be helpful for aspiring business owners. The information, abilities, and network gained by a college education can greatly help an entrepreneur succeed, even though it is not a must for entrepreneurship. College programs frequently offer business management, finance, marketing, and other pertinent courses, giving students the knowledge and skills they need to start and run their own businesses. Additionally, the educational setting fosters an entrepreneurial mindset by encouraging innovation, critical thinking, and problem-solving abilities.

In conclusion, a college degree's worth in the labor market of today depends on a number of variables. A college degree still has a lot of value even though the work market is changing and there is a greater need for specialized abilities. It offers a foundation for learning, intellectual growth, and the acquisition of crucial skills that are highly valued by companies. Additionally, a degree provides beneficial networking possibilities, supports professional development, and opens up a wider choice of job options. To make educated choices about pursuing a college degree, people should take into account the changing job market dynamics, industry needs, and financial factors. The value of a college degree ultimately resides in its capacity to deliver a thorough education, foster the development of transferable skills, and improve people's employability prospects in the contemporary job market.

For many, college is well worth the expense. Not only do you gain valuable life experience and make lifelong connections, but a college degree also offers the following advantages:

College Graduates Earn More Than Non-Graduates

The majority of graduates still find that a college degree pays off despite the escalating cost of post-secondary education. someone with a bachelor's degree typically makes a lot more money than someone with merely a high school education.

How much more exactly? According to a 2019 review of Bureau of Labor Statistics data by Northeastern University, the average unemployment rate for those with high school diplomas is 3.7%, and their median annual pay is $38,792. In contrast, bachelor's degree holders earn an average annual salary of $64,896 and experience a 2.2% unemployment rate.

Graduates from colleges have the potential to make hundreds of thousands more than non-graduates over the course of their lives depending on their specific industries.

The Majority of Jobs Require College Education

In previous generations, middle-class living did not require a college degree. In the years prior to the 1980s, two-thirds of jobs required a high school education or less, according to the Georgetown University Center on Education and the Workforce. That's not the situation anymore. By 2027, 70% of all employment, according to Georgetown University, will require some college degree.

Without a degree on your resume, it could be more challenging to land a high-paying position, and competition for open positions is still tough.

College Graduates Are More Likely to Have Health Insurance

Having high-quality health insurance is crucial for your well-being given the spiraling costs of healthcare. However, it can be excessively expensive to purchase health insurance on your own. The baseline price for single-person insurance purchased through the Health Insurance Marketplace is $462 per month or $5,544 annually, according to the Kaiser Family Foundation.

What relevance does that have to college? You might not be aware of it, but a college degree and access to healthcare are significantly correlated.

College graduates are much more likely than high school graduates to get coverage via their employers, which helps cover their medical expenses. According to CollegeBoard.org, employer-provided insurance was available to 64% of employees with bachelor's degrees and 70% of employees with advanced degrees, but only 52% of employees with high school diplomas were covered by employment plans.

While a four-year degree can be valuable for many students, a bachelor's degree isn't necessary for everyone. Before attending college, make sure you consider the following drawbacks:

You Likely Will Graduate With Student Loan Debt

You probably won't be able to pay the entire cost of college out of your savings or earnings from part-time work due to the steep rise in tuition; rather, you'll need to take out student loans to cover at least some of the cost. The Institute for College Access and Success reports that 62% of 2019 college grads had student debt when they graduated, with an average sum of $28,950.

You might have debt for 10 to 30 years, depending on your repayment strategy for student loans. You could feel pressured to postpone other financial objectives like saving for retirement or purchasing a home because of your minimum monthly payments.

High-Paying Jobs Aren't Guaranteed

Even though a college education is frequently portrayed as a route to success, finding a well-paying job after graduation may be challenging, particularly in light of the coronavirus pandemic, which led to tens of millions of individuals filing jobless claims in 2020.

The National Association of Colleges and Employers estimates that the average beginning wage for college graduates is $51,000. Although most people find it to be a decent wage, many graduates will make less than that. Additionally, you might find it difficult to make ends meet if your student loan debt is substantial and outpaces your salary.

It Can Take More Than Four Years to Graduate

Even though earning a college degree is sometimes portrayed as a path to success, the job market can be more competitive than you might think.

Finding a high-paying job after graduation may be challenging, particularly in light of the coronavirus pandemic, which led to tens of millions of individuals filing jobless claims in 2020.

According to the National Association of Colleges and Employers, the typical beginning wage for college graduates immediately out of school is around $51,000. Even while for the majority that is a decent wage, many graduates will make less. Additionally, it could be difficult for you to get by if your student loan debt is significant and outpaces your salary.

So is a college degree worth it? Not necessarily for everyone. If you decide that attending a four-year school isn't the right decision for you, there are other options you can use to earn a good income. Research shows that 2 in 5 Americans don't see the value in their college degree. This is why choosing the proper education as the path to your career is essential.

What Are Your Alternatives?

Community College

A community college education is far less expensive than a four-year college or university education. The average tuition at an in-district community college is just $3,770, according to CollegeBoard.org.

A community college offers associate's degrees and certificate programs that prepare students for secure employment. For instance, the following professions earn above-average salaries and only call for two-year degrees:

- **Radiation therapist:** $80,160
- **Computer programmer:** $79,840
- **Dental assistant:** $72,910
- **Licensed vocational nurse:** $68,450
- **Telecom installer:** $53,640

Trade School

Hands-on training is offered for a variety of specialized professions at trade schools, vocational schools, or technical colleges. With students graduating in six months to two years, the programs are often far shorter than college degrees.

Attending a trade school is significantly less expensive than a four-year university. Program completion typically costs approximately $33,000.

Trade experts are in higher demand than ever, and you can make a good living pursuing a trade expertise. For instance, the U.S. Bureau of Labor Statistics lists the median earnings for the following trades.

These numbers might be a touch low in some states, but you can earn a lot more money.

- **Electrician:** $56,180
- **Plumber:** $55,160
- **Carpenter:** $48,330
- **Mechanic:** $42,090

Entrepreneurship

If you have a business concept, starting your own company can be a better career choice than going to college. You can choose your own schedule and pay as an entrepreneur. Entrepreneurs make an annual compensation of about $43,000 on average. Depending on their business concept and success rate, many earn significantly more.

Though it may take years for your company to start making a profit, keep in mind that starting your own business can be laborious and difficult. Use the tools provided by the U.S. Small Business Administration to obtain assistance developing your concepts and drafting a business plan.

CHAPTER TWELVE

Digital Skills According to Google

Google holds the belief that a college degree is not a prerequisite for securing a lucrative position in the technology industry.

We all know that digital skills are essential for obtaining work nowadays, and even more so if one wants to make a solid livelihood. Indeed, more than 60% of employment has required either high-level or medium-level computer abilities since the beginning of the last decade. While COVID-19 increased unemployment, people are eager to gain new skills.

Even while higher education is enticing in today's economy, it is expensive and takes a long time (usually 3-5 years of college time) to obtain the necessary expertise. What if people could swiftly learn advanced skills using online learning tools? To prepare for such a scenario, Google offers unique professional credentials that can help people advance their professions and even jumpstart their tech careers in order to get well-paying jobs.

After the covid pandemic, in a blog post, Kent Walker, Senior Vice President of Global Affairs at Google, stated that people should not require a college certificate to be economically secure. "We need new, accessible job-training solutions—from enhanced vocational programs to online education—to help America recover and rebuild," he wrote.

The new Google Career Certificates were built on Google's existing programs to provide those without college degrees with pathways into IT Support employment. This allows people to get job-ready skills in high-demand industries such as data analysis, project management, UX design, and IT support specialist. These certifications, according to Google, also connect learners to top national firms that are hiring for appropriate employment roles.

Mr. Walker went on to say that college degrees are out of reach for many Americans and that innovative, accessible job-training alternatives, ranging from upgraded vocational programs to online education, are needed to help America recover and rebuild.

Is a Google Certificate For You?

Google Career Certificates are designed to be industry-specific and to teach practical skills in high-demand sectors. The IT support, data analytics, and UX design credentials, in particular, appeal to rapidly expanding businesses and need individuals with relevant abilities. Individuals can demonstrate expertise in sought-after fields by obtaining these qualifications, which can improve their career prospects.

Affordability and Accessibility

Google Career Certificates are often less expensive and more accessible than standard degree programs. Certificates are often less expensive and require less time to achieve, making them appealing options for individuals wishing to upskill or explore new professional fields without the limits of a full-time degree program. Furthermore, the online format allows for flexible learning, allowing individuals to study at their own speed while balancing other obligations.

Practical and Job-Focused Training

Google Career Certificates emphasize practical, job-relevant abilities that may be utilized immediately in the workplace. Real-world projects and case studies are frequently incorporated into the curriculum, which is often produced in partnership with industry professionals. This emphasis on practical learning can benefit students who need to acquire specific skills fast and efficiently to fulfill immediate job market demands.

Recognition and Credibility

While Google Career Certificates may not be as well-known as traditional degrees from prestigious universities, they are gaining traction in the industry. The credibility of these certifications is enhanced by Google's brand name and reputation, and many companies value the skills and knowledge provided by Google's training programs. However, it is crucial to remember that the recognition of these qualifications may differ across industries and organizations.

Career Advancement Opportunities

Obtaining a Google Career Certificate can help you succeed in your career. It can lead to entry-level roles, prospects for career shifts, or act as a springboard for future professional growth. However, it is critical to remember that, in addition to the certificate itself, professional advancement frequently depends on a combination of criteria such as experience, abilities, networking, and industry demand.

Continuous Learning and Skill Enhancement

Google Career Certificates have a value that continues beyond the first certification. Google's online learning platform provides constant access to updated knowledge and tools, allowing individuals to stay current with industry trends and improve their abilities over time. This emphasis on lifelong learning is extremely beneficial in today's quickly changing employment environment.

Finally, Google professional Certificates may be worthwhile to obtain depending on an individual's professional aspirations, industry demand, and specific circumstances. They offer low-cost, accessible training in high-demand professions, with an emphasis on practical skills that might improve employability. However, before obtaining a Google Career Certificate, it is critical to evaluate industry recognition, career opportunities, and individual learning needs.

When these qualifications are combined with relevant work experience, networking, and continued professional development, their value can be maximized and contribute to long-term career success.

Since its inception in 2018, the Google IT Certificate program has risen to become one of Coursera's, most well-known certificates. Coursera is a global online learning platform that offers anyone, anywhere, access to online courses and degrees from leading universities and companies.

Google claims that thousands of people have gained new employment and increased their salaries as a result of completing these courses.

Why This Is Important

Google has stated that the certificates offer a route to employment because the tech giant will connect Certificate graduates with top firms in their respective nations. The certifications are intended to prepare students for high-demand, well-paying jobs with a median annual salary of more than $50,000.

Google's certificate classes can be completed in six months. The best thing is that Google has intimated that possessing the certificate might be treated similarly to four-year college degrees.

Because it was created exclusively by Google, it has the potential to be a game changer for anyone wishing to change occupations or enhance their careers. Google awards grants and scholarships to eligible students. Coursera hosts all information connected to courses and specific jobs.

Google, like other career certifications, claims that no degree or prior experience is required. In fact, 61% of enrolled students do not have a four-year degree. This certificate could be an excellent starting point for a career in information technology. Certificate courses are not available for free. In terms of prices, a typical student takes three to six months to complete the certificate program for the IT support curriculum, which costs roughly $49 per month.

Short-term certificates are important because they train people in practical skills in a shorter period of time than a regular college education. Such abilities and certificates can be extremely useful in the resale and continual learning required in the technology business.

Such certifications are not only useful for obtaining specialized skills, but they are also significantly less expensive than standard university degrees. Furthermore, unlike colleges, the curriculum can be altered every year based on the demands of hands-on practical activity.

CHAPTER THIRTEEN
LinkedIn

"Get LinkedIn or Get Left Out"

— THE INTERVIEW MINDSET BY MARK JAMES

Back in late 2015, when I was asked to join the Advisory Board of the College of Business at California State University San Marcos, I felt both honored and privileged. Then Dean, Dr. Jim Hamerly then requested that I work with him and six other CEOs to develop a business professional development course. This was followed by the development of the Executive in Residence Program. Seven executives were tasked with developing the curriculum, which would enable our business graduates to launch their professions. The objective of this project was to provide the students with all the hard and soft skills needed to not only get employment but also to land the job they desired.

The Outcomes We Were Looking For.

Upon the successful completion of this course, each student would then be able to:

- Develop an effective resume and cover letter
- Develop and professionally use LinkedIn
- Explain the attributes of an effective team member
- Effectively and professionally network with others by conducting informational interviews
- Effectively and professionally perform in a job interview
- Develop and deliver an effective oral presentation
- Develop an individual career development plan

Why Business Professional Development?

On average, it takes college graduates 6-9 months to find a job. Pursuing an alternative career outcome (e.g., startup, graduate school, military, volunteer, etc.) generally takes on average a year or more of planning and execution. We felt as a group, that determining a post-graduation career path prior to graduation was the key to improving *the student's chances of success.*

Today, employers start recruiting students as early as the fall semester of their sophomore year for summer internships and future employment. The largest recruiting season for seniors is the fall semester prior to graduation. The course we created strongly emphasizes the importance of how to effectively network to improve career outcomes and how to DIFFERENTIATE yourself from other future graduates.

The Business Professional Development course was designed to help students achieve their career goals by enhancing their soft skills and occupational search strategies. Networking is a major factor in gaining employment and improving your knowledge of industries and trends.

The same holds true for people in transition or in the process of re-creating themselves.

Why LinkedIn Is Important

As my friend and colleague Mark James points out in his book, The Interview Mindset, "If you don't embrace LinkedIn at every stage of your career, you are dead in the water."

There are many ways to grow your professional network, but LinkedIn is by far one of the easiest paths to take. LinkedIn has 830 million members in more than 200 countries and territories worldwide. The mission of LinkedIn is simple: connect the world's professionals to make them more productive and successful.

According to one of America's top career coaches, Robin Ryan, "94% of all recruiters spend at least an hour or two on LinkedIn every day and when they are looking for talent". She goes on to state that "To be effective, your profile cannot just be a copy and paste of your resume or just a simple uncompleted profile."

In the old days, the art of connecting was on display in person. It played to our social sensibilities at the bar or over a cup of coffee. While those forms of connection are still important today (especially in a post-pandemic world), professional networks like LinkedIn can approximate traditional networking and empower people to reach brand-new audiences worldwide. You're not confined to the cafe next door or the bar nearby—the world is literally your oyster.

Most people understand that networking is important to career success, but many fail to harness the full power of LinkedIn.

Building Your LinkedIn Page

Jane Deehan, Senior Content Marketing Manager at LinkedIn, has provided the following advice.

"Your personal branding is built on the basis of your LinkedIn profile page. Additionally, LinkedIn frequently introduces new features to expand its functionality as a platform for personal marketing and offer fresh ways to communicate motives and skill sets. You can discover fresh opportunities to develop your personal brand if you haven't lately visited your profile page."

Here are 19 profile hints that you need to review and apply to your profile. Some of them are extremely easy wins, while others could take some time, but they are all well worth the effort. Your personal brand and LinkedIn profile will benefit from their assistance.

1. *Choose the right profile picture for LinkedIn.*

Your profile image is your calling card on LinkedIn; it's how people are introduced to you, and (being the visual creatures that we are), it dictates their first impressions. To begin, here are some simple pointers: Make sure the photo is recent and looks like you, that your face fills up roughly 60% of the photo (long-distance images don't stand out), and that you're wearing what you'd like to wear to work. Make an effort to grin with your eyes.

2. *Add a background photo.*

Your background photo is the second visual element at the top of your profile page. It catches people's attention, establishes the context, and reveals a little more about what's important to you. Above all, the correct background photo makes your page stand out, engage attention, and remain remembered.

3. *Make your headline more than just a job title.*

There is no restriction stating that the description at the top of your profile page must only be a job title. Use the headline field to elaborate on how you see your role, why you do what you do, and what motivates you. If you have sales reps at your organization that are on top of social selling, look at their profile page headlines for ideas. They will almost definitely include more than just their job titles.

4. *Turn your summary into your story.*

The first thing to mention about your LinkedIn synopsis is that you should have one. It's incredible how many people still leave this field empty when building their LinkedIn profiles. Your summary is your opportunity to convey your own story, so don't just list your talents or work titles. Try to explain why those talents are important - and how they can help the people you work with. Don't be afraid to put in some effort, attempt a few revisions, and run your summary by individuals you know. This is your most personal piece of content marketing, and it is well worth your time.

5. Eliminate overused buzzwords.

Buzzwords are adjectives that appear so frequently in LinkedIn headlines and summaries that they have almost no meaning. Terms like specialized,' 'leadership,' 'focused, 'strategic,' 'experienced,' 'passionate,' 'expert,' 'creative,' 'innovation,' and 'certified' appear on LinkedIn's regular list of the most over-used buzzwords. Simply saying these phrases will not persuade others that you possess these qualities. You must also display them in how you describe yourself and use LinkedIn profile elements to convey what you're about.

6. Grow your network.

Syncing your LinkedIn profile with your email address book is one of the simplest and most effective ways to expand your LinkedIn network. This allows LinkedIn to recommend people for you to connect with. It's incredible how effective this can be at surfacing relevant people for you to contact - yet no connection requests are issued without your approval, allowing you to assess all possible connections. Aside from that, make a habit of following up on meetings and conversations with LinkedIn connection requests - it's a terrific way to keep your network vibrant and up to date.

7. List your relevant skills.

It's one of LinkedIn's quickest wins: go through the list of skills and identify ones that are relevant to you. This helps to substantiate the description in your Headline and Summary and gives others a platform to recommend you. The goal here, however, is to remain relevant. A big list of abilities that aren't fundamental to who you are and what you do might become overwhelming. Update your skill list on a regular basis.

8. *Emphasize the services you provide.*

Services is a new LinkedIn feature that allows consultants, freelancers, and people working for small businesses to promote the services they provide. Filling out your profile's Services section might increase your exposure in search results.

9. *Spread the endorsement, love.*

Endorsements from other members validate your abilities and boost your credibility. How can you get your LinkedIn profile endorsed? To begin, browse through your network and choose connections that you believe truly merit your recommendation - this is typically the trigger for individuals to return the favor. Don't be scared to send a courteous message asking for approval for a few crucial talents as well. But keep in mind that relevancy is important. Contact people whose approval you highly value.

10. *Manage your endorsements more proactively.*

Once you start receiving endorsements, you may see that they tilt the emphasis of your LinkedIn profile in ways that do not reflect who you are. It's possible that your primary area of expertise is content marketing, but those who have worked with you on events are more enthusiastic supporters. Use the edit features in the Skills part of your profile to manage the list of your endorsements - you can pick which to show and which to hide.

11. *Take a skills assessment.*

An online skills evaluation allows you to demonstrate the degree of your skills and display a Verified Skills badge on your profile. According to data, candidates with verified skills are approximately 30% more likely to get hired for the roles they apply for - and providing proof of your expertise boosts your personal brand more broadly. Displaying the results of your skills assessments is completely optional, and you can retake the tests as many times as you like before indicating that you've passed.

12. Request recommendations.

Endorsements give visitors to your profile a fast, visual idea of what you're recognized for. Recommendations take things to the next level. They are written personal testimonials that demonstrate the experience of working with you. Your profile's Recommendations section has a useful drop-down menu that allows you to reach out to specific contacts and request recommendations. Consider whom you would most value a recommendation from - then customize your request. It is well worth the extra work.

13. Showcase your passion for learning

When you finish a course on LinkedIn Learning, you will be able to add a course certificate to your LinkedIn profile. This is done through the Learning History area of your LinkedIn Learning account, where you can also choose to broadcast updates about your learning to your network.

14. Share media and marketing collateral.

The marketing collateral you create for your company might also help you raise your own profile. Sharing case studies, white papers, and other brand content helps to demonstrate what your company is all about - and helps people understand what makes you tick. It also exhibits enthusiasm and devotion.

15. Get credit for your thought leadership with Publications.

The Publications section is one of the most under-used elements in LinkedIn profiles – and that means that you can really stand out from the crowd when you use this feature to draw attention to existing thought-leadership content. Have you helped to write an eBook or a

White Paper? Or write a post on your company's blog? The Publications section links your profile to these assets.

16. Share relevant content from your LinkedIn feed.

It's one thing to have a network of LinkedIn connections; it's far better to play an active part in that network, appearing in your contacts' LinkedIn feeds in a way that provides value to their lives. Sharing relevant content with your network is one of the simplest methods to accomplish this. Start by monitoring your LinkedIn feed and posting stuff that you find really fascinating - and that matches your point of view.

17. Add comments.

Sharing is wonderful, but it is only the beginning. When you leave comments on your shares, you give yourself more visibility in the stream and begin to convey why you believe a certain piece of material is important. Well-written comments also allow you to share a wider range of topics. It's possible that you disagree with a point of view yet still find it interesting. A comment expressing that point of view develops your opinion and thought leadership. It's also more likely to elicit more comments, which will enhance your LinkedIn profile. Keep this in mind while you write your comment, and make sure you're saying something you're comfortable with others associating with you.

18. Follow relevant influencers for your industry.

Following relevant influencers on LinkedIn helps to populate your feed with a variety of intriguing items, which you can subsequently share with others when you believe it adds value. It also adds context to your LinkedIn profile, displaying your enthusiasm for what you do.

19. Publish long-form content – and use it to start conversations.

The more you share and comment on information, the more your expertise and thought-leadership credentials will be established on LinkedIn. The inevitable next step is to publish long-form posts. Monitoring the response to your comments and shares is a good place to start. Are there any topics or points of view that appear to resonate with your network? Are there any comments you've made that you think you could build on in a post? Evolving your thought leadership in this way maintains its authenticity - and keeps you connected to the problems your contacts are discussing. Be prepared for your long-form posts to spark fresh discussions. Maintain an eye on the comments and be prepared to answer.

Getting your LinkedIn profile working harder for you doesn't have to take up hours of your time. Try working through these ideas, building from one to the other. You'll that you can make progress quickly, even if you're just able to set aside a few minutes each day.

Seven LinkedIn Mistakes to Avoid.

There has been a tendency in the past for Baby Boomers, Gen. Xers, and even some Gen Y's to ignore LinkedIn. A number of my current students refuse to embrace it. Eventually, they realize that there are beneficial returns for creating a profile on LinkedIn and using LinkedIn's network to job hunt. Here are some mistakes you want to avoid or correct.

1. **Make sure you have a full profile**. A complete, full profile is essential if you want to be found on LinkedIn. Make sure you fill out all the sections correctly, and don't ignore any of the areas.
2. **Work experience**. Many people have relatively little amount of work experience. The job title, employer name,

and dates of employment are all listed. Others may have lengthy or generic job descriptions. Another common blunder is describing what the company does rather than what they do. The work history is an important component. It's frequently sifted through by recruiters attempting to poach an employer and get you interested in one of their employment openings. So, in the Experience section, you'll want to highlight a few notable accomplishments and results from that work. Recent roles are more important than roles from 15 or more years ago. In fact, I make it a point to advise them not to go back more than ten years. There is far too much potential for age discrimination.

3. **Poor headline**. People underestimate the significance of selecting compelling keywords for their headlines. Many people claim they had no idea they could or should update their headline. When you check under your name, LinkedIn automatically generates your headline, which simply lists your current work title. Job titles that describe roles you have held or aspire to should be included in the headline. In addition, you can highlight a specialty, such as eCommerce specialist, or certification, such as Scrum Master.

4. **Not being active on LinkedIn**. The more you post on LinkedIn, the better you will fare with the website's algorithm. Keep in mind that posting is not the same as leaving a remark or like anything. Posting entails publishing original content, posing a question to your network, conducting a poll, or sharing an article that you believe will be useful to other connections. According to LinkedIn, posting once a day, five days a week, will significantly improve the amount of individuals who see your profile. Finding content to post about five days a week, though, can be challenging. A weekly posting schedule would be preferable. Discuss business news or industry challenges. Sharing a pertinent article you read gets easier and more

doable after that. Finding stories quickly can be done by scanning the news feed on your phone. Searching for items on a news aggregator like the Flipboard app is a great alternative technique. You can customize the content that displays in magazine format with this software. By selecting the topics you want to read about and then quickly locating an article to share, you may customize the articles you receive. The biggest benefit is that submitting an existing article takes much less time than creating original content.

5. **The "about" section.** Use the first sentence to succinctly convey your experience. Then things get personal. Skills and job history are available elsewhere. LinkedIn suggests that you use this section to express your personality. You can describe what kind of boss you are. Keep the information personal and write in a welcoming tone. Personal information such as marriage, three children, and so on should not be included.

6. **You have few if any, connections.** The number of connections you have affects your visibility on our platform. People with fewer than 75 connections are at a severe disadvantage. LinkedIn suggests having 300-500 contacts for a strong network. Try to contact friends, coworkers, past bosses, college pals, former coworkers, and so on. The first step is to expand your network.

7. **Unflattering photo.** It never ceases to amaze me the terrible photos some people use on LinkedIn. This is your personal brand. Using a lousy photo is not marketing yourself in the best possible light. Skip using a picture that is obviously clipped from a party, wedding, family function, or some casual event. Nothing is more important than showing a professional-looking headshot with a smiling face that looks warm and engaging. You don't necessarily need a professional photographer. You can get a high-enough

quality picture using your cell phone. As stated previously, if your image is more than two years old, you need a new one. `

Additional Suggestions for Your LinkedIn Site

Consider your LinkedIn page to be a business. Most people consider their LinkedIn profile to be an online CV, a place where they may demonstrate their skills and expertise to potential employers. If you want to get the most out of LinkedIn, you must be aggressive in obtaining views. Consider your profile to be a business that you must aggressively sell. This concept is the foundation for many other suggestions on the list.

Remember to use keywords to increase your visibility. Most recruiters and LinkedIn users identify their ideal candidates by searching for certain terms. For example, a recruiter looking for a marketing manager for a tech company would presumably type "marketing manager tech" or something similar into the search field and go at a couple of the profiles that showed up as suggestions. Remember to include the most relevant keywords to the role you seek in your title, synopsis, employment experience, and postings (if you're actively posting).

CHAPTER FOURTEEN
The Resume

"The most valuable of all talents is that of never using two words when one will do."

— THOMAS JEFFERSON

I've either created or assisted in creating thousands of resumes for people throughout the years. I have written resumes for students, members of my family, close friends, and coworkers who needed help getting the job they really desired. I've used a variety of software programs, including Vmock, which is, in my opinion, the best.

When it comes to writing a resume, there are several universal rules that can help you create a strong and effective document. While the specific content and formatting may vary depending on your industry and individual circumstances, the following 13 rules apply to most resumes:

1. Keep it concise.

Resumes should be concise and focused. Aim for a one or two-page document that highlights your most relevant skills, experiences, and qualifications. Use bullet points and concise phrases to convey information efficiently.

2. Use a professional format and layout.

Choose a clean and professional resume format that is easy to read and navigate. Use a consistent font style and size throughout the document, and ensure proper spacing and margins. Use headings and subheadings to organize different sections of your resume.

3. Include relevant contact information.

Provide your full name, professional email address, and phone number. If applicable, include a link to your LinkedIn profile or personal website/portfolio. Exclude unnecessary personal information such as your date of birth or marital status.

4. Write a compelling summary or objective statement.

Begin your resume with a strong summary or objective statement that provides a concise overview of your skills, experiences, and career goals. Tailor this statement to match the specific job or industry you are targeting.

5. Highlight your most relevant skills.

Create a dedicated skills section that lists your key skills and areas of expertise. Be sure to include both hard skills (technical abilities) and soft skills (interpersonal and communication skills) that are relevant to the job you're applying for.

6. Emphasize your work experience.

Include a section that outlines your work experience in reverse chronological order (starting with your most recent position). For each job, include the company name, job title, dates of employment, and a bulleted list of your key responsibilities and achievements.

7. Quantify achievements and results.

Whenever possible, include specific achievements, metrics, or results to demonstrate the impact of your work. Quantifying your accomplishments adds credibility and helps employers understand the value you can bring to their organization.

8. Include relevant educational background.

List your educational qualifications, starting with the most recent. Include the name of the institution, degree earned, and dates of attendance. If you have limited work experience, highlight relevant coursework, projects, or academic achievements.

9. Tailor your resume to the job.

Customize your resume for each job application to highlight the skills and experiences most relevant to the specific role. Analyze the job description and incorporate keywords and phrases that align with the requirements of the position.

10. Proofread and edit carefully.

Review your resume multiple times to ensure it is free of grammatical errors, typos, and inconsistencies. Use a spell-check tool and ask someone else to review it for you. A well-polished resume demonstrates attention to detail and professionalism.

11. Be honest and truthful.

Always be honest and truthful in your resume. Represent your skills, experiences, and qualifications accurately. Misrepresenting or exaggerating information can harm your reputation and lead to negative consequences if discovered.

12. Use action verbs and power words.

Begin each bullet point under your work experience section with an action verb to describe your accomplishments and responsibilities. This adds impact and creates a dynamic tone. Examples of action verbs include "implemented," "managed," "achieved," and "collaborated."

13. Tailor your resume for digital applications.

In today's digital age, many resumes are submitted electronically or scanned by applicant tracking systems (ATS). Ensure your resume is compatible with ATS by using standard fonts, avoiding excessive formatting, and optimizing keywords for the specific job application.

Remember that these principles are meant to be basic recommendations, so it's necessary to modify them to fit your unique situation and accepted practices in your business. Create a resume that is specific to you in order to highlight your special qualifications and stand out as a good applicant for the position you're applying for.

The following are tips and suggestions I have put together over the years. Many come from sites like LinkedIn, Indeed, Monster, Glassdoor, and Ladders.

- Remember that a CV serves as a first impression. Initial impressions and first impressions are often lasting impressions.
- Your resume will be delivered with numerous others, necessitating a rapid review or use of an internet keyword search engine. How can you get yours to stand out?
- Sloppy or incorrect resumes will be rejected.
- The recruiter is looking to see if the applicant has the necessary abilities and background to execute the job. Your resume should answer the three following questions.

1. Is the applicant capable of completing tasks?
2. Is the resume suited to my particular job?
3. Does it demonstrate genuine interest and research?

Resume Check List

Formal Name of Resume: Make sure your resume is named properly. Example: John Paul Jones Resume 2022. Docx.

Heading: Your name should be capitalized and bold with all your contact information listed.

Objective: Does it list a specific position? (It is okay to have multiple resumes.

Summary: Does your resume show demonstrated experience?

Education: List School, degree, major, and graduation date ONLY if you have been out of school for less than 10 years. Once you are out of school for more than two are three years, your grade point average is irrelevant. List relevant courses if tailoring your resume for a specific job.

Work Experience: Job title, company name, city/state, dates worked.

(*List accomplishments with Action Verbs.....see below*)

Formatting and Grammar: Consistent, error-free, no typos, punctuation checked, good formatting, and list in reverse chronological order.

Action verbs are words that express an action. In a resume, action verbs are used to highlight your skills, experience, and accomplishments. They are specific, clarify your contributions and bring a confident tone to your resume. Using action verbs that are unique and powerful can increase your chances of capturing the attention of an employer and moving to the next step in the hiring process. Here's an example:

Six Universal Rules for Resume Writing

1. Cover all the basics.
2. Explore other resumes for inspiration.
3. Use as few words as possible.
4. Quantify your accomplishments whenever possible.
5. Use keywords that employers are using in their job descriptions.
6. Proofread several times to catch typos and misspellings.

Use action verbs.

Words that express an activity are known as action verbs. Action verbs are employed in resumes to highlight your talents, experience, and accomplishments. They are specific, define your contributions, and give your CV a confident tone. Using distinctive and compelling action verbs can boost your chances of attracting an employer's attention and progressing to the next level in the hiring process.

Here's an example:

Wrong: Lacks strength and clarity: *"Held weekly status meetings to share client updates."*

Right: Empowered and detailed: *"Spearheaded weekly status meetings to communicate agency revenue growth."*

You can see how the second option is stronger and more detailed. The action verbs make your contribution clear and impactful.

Professional tip: Combine your selection of action verbs with quantifiable results to show both what you did and the effect it had. For example, *"Championed use of user feedback in program improvements, resulting in 50% boost in customer satisfaction ratings."*

Here are some good resume action verbs you can use to showcase your accomplishments.

1. Achieved

Demonstrated successful outcomes or results. Example: "Achieved a sales target of $1 million within six months."

2. Improved

Enhanced or made positive changes to a process, system, or situation. Example: "Improved customer satisfaction ratings by 20% through the implementation of a new feedback system."

3. Initiated

Took the lead or started a project, program, or initiative. Example: "Initiated and led a cross-functional team to develop and launch a new product line."

4. Generated

Created or produced something, such as revenue, leads, or ideas. Example: "Generated $500,000 in additional revenue through strategic partnerships."

5. Implemented

Executed or put into action a plan, strategy, or solution. Example: "Implemented a streamlined inventory management system, reducing costs by 15%."

6. Streamlined

Made a process more efficient or simplified it. Example: "Streamlined the recruitment process, reducing time-to-hire by 30%."

7. Resolved

Successfully solved a problem or conflict. Example: "Resolved customer complaints, resulting in a 20% decrease in customer escalations."

8. Innovated

Introduced new ideas, methods, or technologies. Example: "Innovated a new software feature that improved user experience and increased customer retention by 25%."

9. Led

Guided or supervised a team or project. Example: "Led a team of 10 engineers to develop and launch a new mobile application."

10. Optimized

Made improvements to enhance performance, efficiency, or effectiveness. Example: "Optimized website loading time, resulting in a 40% decrease in bounce rate."

Remember to tailor the action verbs to your specific achievements and use them consistently throughout your resume to create a powerful and impactful document.

Action verbs to explain responsibilities:

When explaining your responsibilities on a resume, it's important to use action verbs that convey a sense of proactivity and achievement. Here are some effective action verbs to describe responsibilities:

1. Managed

Oversaw and guided a team or project. Example: "Managed a team of 15 employees and coordinated daily operations."

2. Coordinated

Organized and synchronized various elements or activities. Example: "Coordinated logistics for company events, including venue selection, vendor negotiation, and attendee management."

3. Implemented

Executed or put into action a plan, strategy, or process. Example: "Implemented a new performance evaluation system to enhance employee development and engagement."

4. Developed

Created or enhanced something, such as skills, programs, or relationships. Example: "Developed and delivered training programs to enhance employee productivity and performance."

5. Conducted

Carried out research, analysis, or investigations. Example: "Conducted market research to identify customer needs and preferences for new product development."

6. Oversaw

Supervised or monitored a process, department, or project. Example: "Oversaw the financial operations of a $5 million budget and ensured compliance with accounting standards."

7. Collaborated

Worked closely with others to achieve common goals. Example: "Collaborated with cross-functional teams to develop and launch a new marketing campaign."

8. Analyzed

Examined data or information to derive insights or make informed decisions. Example: "Analyzed sales trends and customer behavior to identify opportunities for revenue growth."

9. Established

Created or set up a process, protocol, or relationship. Example: "Established and maintained strategic partnerships with key clients to drive business growth."

Remember to use these action verbs to start your bullet points and provide specific examples and results to demonstrate your impact and achievements in each responsibility.

Action verbs to express communication skills:

When highlighting your communication skills on a resume, incorporating strong action verbs can effectively convey your abilities in this area. Here are some action verbs to express communication skills:

1. Communicated

Conveyed information, ideas, or messages effectively. Example: "Communicated project updates and milestones to team members and stakeholders."

2. Presented

Delivered information, reports, or proposals to individuals or groups. Example: "Presented sales strategies to executive leadership, resulting in a 20% increase in revenue."

3. Facilitated

Guided or led discussions, meetings, or workshops. Example: "Facilitated team brainstorming sessions to generate innovative ideas."

4. Negotiated

Engaged in discussions to reach mutually beneficial agreements. Example: "Negotiated contracts with vendors, achieving cost savings of 15%."

5. Persuaded

Convinced or influenced others to adopt a particular viewpoint or take action. Example: "Persuaded clients to implement recommended solutions, resulting in improved operational efficiency."

6. Mediated

Assisted in resolving conflicts or disputes between individuals or groups. Example: "Mediated team conflicts, fostering a more collaborative work environment."

7. Liaised

Acted as a point of contact and maintained effective communication between different parties. Example: "Liaised with cross-functional teams to ensure seamless project execution."

8. Clarified

Made information or instructions clear and understandable. Example: "Clarified complex technical concepts for non-technical stakeholders."

9. Listened

Actively paid attention and understood information conveyed by others. Example: "Listened attentively to customer feedback, identifying areas for improvement and addressing concerns."

10. Corresponded

Exchanged written communication through emails, letters, or memos. Example: "Corresponded with clients to address inquiries and provide timely responses."

Remember to provide specific examples of how you effectively utilized these communication skills to achieve positive outcomes in your previous roles. By incorporating these action verbs, you can effectively showcase your strong communication skills to potential employee

Action verbs for creative experience:

When highlighting your creative experience on a resume, it's important to use action verbs that showcase your ability to think innovatively, generate ideas, and produce unique solutions. Here are some action verbs to demonstrate creative experience:

1. Conceptualized

Generated or developed new ideas, concepts, or strategies. Example: "Conceptualized and designed a new product line targeting a younger demographic."

2. Designed

Created or developed visually appealing and functional designs. Example: "Designed user interfaces for mobile applications, focusing on intuitive navigation and seamless user experience."

3. Innovated

Introduced new ideas, methods, or technologies. Example: "Innovated a cost-effective manufacturing process, resulting in a 30% reduction in production time."

4. Created

Produced or developed original content, artwork, or designs. Example: "Created engaging social media campaigns, resulting in a 50% increase in follower engagement."

5. Developed

Generated or improved upon existing ideas, concepts, or products. Example: "Developed a new marketing strategy to target niche markets and increase brand visibility."

6. Brainstormed

Collaborated with others to generate creative ideas and solutions. Example: "Brainstormed with a team of designers to create innovative packaging concepts for a new product launch."

7. Illustrated

Created visual representations or artwork to convey ideas or concepts. Example: "Illustrated a series of children's books, bringing characters to life through vibrant and captivating illustrations."

8. Curated

Selected and organized content or materials to create a cohesive and impactful experience. Example: "Curated an art exhibition featuring emerging artists, showcasing a diverse range of styles and mediums."

9. Adapted

Modified or customized existing ideas or designs to fit specific requirements. Example: "Adapted website templates to create unique and visually appealing designs for clients."

10. Explored

Explored new approaches, techniques, or possibilities. Example: "Explored alternative materials and production methods to create sustainable and eco-friendly products."

Remember to provide specific examples of your creative experience and the outcomes you achieved through your creative contributions.

Using these action verbs will help highlight your ability to think outside the box, generate innovative ideas, and contribute creatively to projects and initiatives.

Action verbs for sales experience:

When describing your sales experience on a resume, it's crucial to use action verbs that convey your ability to drive revenue, build relationships, and achieve sales targets. Here are some action verbs that demonstrate sales experience effectively:

1. Generated

Produced or created leads, opportunities, or revenue. Example: "Generated $1 million in sales revenue within the first quarter."

2. Prospected

Identified and pursued potential customers or clients. Example: "Prospected and secured new clients, resulting in a 20% increase in customer base."

3. Closed

Successfully finalized sales or deals. Example: "Closed high-value contracts with key accounts, exceeding monthly sales targets."

4. Consulted

Provided expert advice and guidance to clients, understanding their needs and recommending appropriate solutions. Example: "Consulted with clients to assess their requirements and tailor product offerings to their specific needs."

5. Negotiated

Engaged in discussions to reach mutually beneficial agreements. Example: "Negotiated pricing and contract terms to secure long-term partnerships with major clients."

6. Presented

Delivered compelling sales presentations to showcase products or services. Example: "Presented product demonstrations to potential clients, resulting in a 30% increase in sales conversions."

7. Upsold

Suggested additional products or services to enhance the customer's purchase. Example: "Upsold premium features to customers, increasing the average transaction value by 25%."

8. Built

Developed and fostered strong relationships with clients or accounts. Example: "Built a solid network of strategic partnerships, leading to a 40% increase in referral business."

9. Exceeded

Surpassed sales targets or quotas. Example: "Exceeded quarterly sales targets by 15%, consistently ranking as a top performer within the sales team."

10. Managed

Oversaw and nurtured customer accounts or territories. Example: "Managed a portfolio of 50+ accounts, consistently driving customer satisfaction and repeat business."

Remember to quantify your achievements with specific numbers and percentages whenever possible to showcase the impact of your sales efforts. These action verbs will help demonstrate your sales expertise and highlight your ability to drive results, build relationships, and close deals effectively.

Action verbs for leadership and management:

When emphasizing your leadership and management skills on a resume, it's important to use action verbs that convey your ability to guide, motivate, and oversee teams or projects. Here are some of the best action verbs to showcase your leadership and management experience:

1. Led

Guided, directed, or supervised a team or project. Example: "Led a cross-functional team of 15 members to launch a new product successfully."

2. Managed

Oversaw and coordinated the activities of a team or department. Example: "Managed a team of sales representatives, achieving a 20% increase in quarterly revenue."

3. Directed

Provided clear instructions and guidance to individuals or groups. Example: "Directed the implementation of a new company-wide training program."

4. Mentored

Offered guidance, support, and coaching to team members. Example: "Mentored junior employees, fostering their professional growth and development."

5. Delegated

Assigned tasks or responsibilities to team members based on their strengths and abilities. Example: "Delegated project tasks effectively, optimizing team productivity and efficiency."

6. Inspired

Motivated and encouraged team members to achieve their full potential. Example: "Inspired a high-performance culture within the team, resulting in increased employee engagement and productivity."

7. Streamlined

Improved processes, workflows, or systems to enhance efficiency and effectiveness. Example: "Streamlined operational procedures, reducing costs by 15% and improving overall efficiency."

8. Implemented

Executed or put into action strategies, initiatives, or programs. Example: "Implemented a new performance management system, resulting in improved employee performance and retention."

9. Coordinated

Organized and synchronized various elements or activities to achieve a common goal. Example: "Coordinated the launch of a new marketing campaign across multiple channels."

10. Influenced

Persuaded or shaped the opinions and actions of others to achieve desired outcomes. Example: "Influenced key stakeholders to adopt a new strategic direction, resulting in increased market share."

Remember to provide specific examples and quantifiable achievements that highlight your leadership and management capabilities. By incorporating these action verbs, you can effectively demonstrate your ability to lead teams, drive projects, and achieve results.

Action verbs for experience with finance:

When highlighting your experience with finance on a resume, it's important to use action verbs that demonstrate your ability to analyze financial data, make informed decisions, and drive financial outcomes. Here are some of the best action verbs to showcase your finance experience:

1. Analyzed

Examined and interpreted financial data to derive insights and make informed decisions. Example: "Analyzed financial statements to identify cost-saving opportunities and improve profitability."

2. Managed

Oversaw and coordinated financial operations, budgets, or projects. Example: "Managed a $1 million budget, ensuring cost control and adherence to financial guidelines."

3. Forecasted

Predicted or projected financial trends, outcomes, or performance. Example: "Forecasted cash flow and revenue projections, facilitating effective resource allocation and budget planning."

4. Evaluated

Assessed or reviewed financial performance, risks, or investment opportunities. Example: "Evaluated investment portfolios and recommended asset allocation strategies to optimize returns."

5. Implemented

Executed or put into action financial strategies, policies, or systems. Example: "Implemented a new expense tracking system, resulting in improved accuracy and timeliness of financial reporting."

6. Audited

Examined financial records and processes to ensure compliance and accuracy. Example: "Audited internal controls and financial statements to ensure regulatory compliance and minimize risks."

7. Optimized

Improved financial efficiency, profitability, or processes. Example: "Optimized inventory management practices, reducing carrying costs by 20% while maintaining product availability."

8. Negotiated

Engaged in discussions to reach favorable financial agreements or terms. Example: "Negotiated vendor contracts to secure cost savings of 15% on key supplies and services."

9. Strategized

Developed financial strategies, plans, or recommendations to achieve business objectives. Example: "Strategized and implemented a pricing model that increased profit margins by 10%."

10. Collaborated

Worked closely with cross-functional teams or stakeholders to achieve financial goals. Example: "Collaborated with sales and marketing teams to develop and execute pricing strategies that drove revenue growth."

Remember to provide specific examples and quantify your achievements whenever possible to showcase the impact of your finance expertise. Using these action verbs will help demonstrate your proficiency in financial analysis, management, and decision-making on your resume.

Action verbs for technical experience:

When highlighting your technical experience on a resume, it's important to use action verbs that demonstrate your proficiency in technical skills, problem-solving abilities, and your capacity to deliver successful outcomes. Here are some of the best action verbs to showcase your technical experience:

1. Developed

Created or built new software, applications, systems, or solutions. Example: "Developed a mobile app that received over 100,000 downloads within the first month of launch."

2. Programmed

Coded or programmed software, websites, or algorithms. Example: "Programmed a web application using HTML, CSS, and JavaScript to enhance user experience."

3. Implemented

Executed or put into action technical solutions, projects, or processes. Example: "Implemented a network security system to protect sensitive data and mitigate cyber threats."

4. Troubleshoot

Identified and resolved technical issues, bugs, or problems. Example: "Troubleshot software defects, reducing system downtime by 30% and improving user satisfaction."

5. Optimized

Enhanced performance, efficiency, or functionality of systems, processes, or websites. Example: "Optimized database queries, resulting in a 20% improvement in application response time."

6. Configured

Set up or customized software, hardware, or network settings. Example: "Configured network infrastructure for a new office location, ensuring seamless connectivity."

7. Collaborated

Worked closely with teams or stakeholders to achieve technical goals or project milestones. Example: "Collaborated with cross-functional teams to develop and launch a new e-commerce platform."

8. Integrated

Combined or merged different systems, technologies, or components. Example: "Integrated third-party APIs to enhance functionality and user experience of the software application."

9. Automated

Implemented automated processes or scripts to streamline workflows or repetitive tasks. Example: "Automated data entry procedures, reducing manual errors by 50% and saving 10 hours per week."

10. Researched

Conducted in-depth research to gather technical information, trends, or best practices. Example: "Researched emerging technologies and recommended a cloud migration strategy to improve scalability."

Remember to tailor these action verbs to your specific technical experiences and accomplishments. Be sure to provide specific examples and quantify your achievements whenever possible to demonstrate the impact of your technical expertise on your resume.

Reminder:

- Your resume needs to show you're a fit for the position
- Good resumes help you land an interview
- DO NOT ADD "References Available Upon Request".
- Objectives are optional; a summary of key qualifications at the top is preferred. (This helps you remember to tailor each resume.)
- Keywords are essential. (Many employers utilize Applicant Tracking Systems (ATS) software. ATS is used by companies of all sizes to organize, search, and communicate with large groups of applicants. Ninety-nine percent of Fortune 500 companies use an ATS as part of their recruiting strategy. We will discuss this later on in the book.)

CHAPTER FIFTEEN
The Cover Letter

I'm always surprised by the number of people who do not submit a cover letter along with their resumes. Over the years, I have seen young and old be eliminated from job consideration due to the lack of a cover letter.

While doing my research, I have spoken to a number of human resources people, hiring managers, and principals who have flatly stated that if they don't see a cover letter accompanying a resume, the resume is either deleted or thrown in the trash can.

The Cover Letter is the perfect tool to customize your Objective to the job's description. It shows your interest and provides specific examples of a position fit while demonstrating your written communication skills.

A well-written cover letter creates a good first impression and can considerably increase an applicant's chances of winning an interview and, eventually, the desired job. This chapter discusses the significance of cover letters in the job application process, emphasizing their capacity to convey qualifications, indicate motivation, emphasize personality, and supplement the resume.

1. Conveying Qualifications

One of the primary purposes of a cover letter is to provide an opportunity for applicants to articulate their qualifications and relevant experiences in a more personalized manner than a resume allows. While a resume offers a concise overview of skills and accomplishments, a cover letter allows candidates to expand upon *specific achievements* and connect them directly to the requirements of the job. By effectively highlighting key qualifications, such as *education, work experience, and technical skills*, cover letters help recruiters understand the applicant's suitability for the position and differentiate themselves from other candidates.

2. Demonstrating Motivation

A well-written cover letter demonstrates genuine interest and motivation for the specific job and company. It provides an avenue for candidates to explain why they are drawn to the role and how their skills align with the organization's goals and values. By showcasing a clear understanding of the company's mission, industry, and culture, applicants can convey their enthusiasm and dedication, setting themselves apart from those who submit generic applications. Moreover, an effective cover letter can convey a proactive attitude, as candidates can explain how they can contribute to the company's success and address specific challenges or opportunities.

3. Showcasing Personality

Beyond qualifications and motivation, a cover letter allows candidates to inject personality into their application. While resumes tend to be formal and structured, cover letters provide an opportunity to showcase individuality, creativity, and communication skills. By adopting an appropriate tone and language, candidates can convey their professional demeanor while expressing their authentic selves. This personal touch helps humanize the application, enabling employers to gauge cultural fit and compatibility with the team. A compelling cover letter not only captures attention but also creates a memorable impression, potentially leading to a deeper connection between the candidate and the employer.

4. Complementing the Resume

While a resume serves as a comprehensive summary of an individual's qualifications and experiences, it often follows a standardized format and may not provide sufficient context for employers.

Here, the cover letter plays a vital role by filling in the gaps and offering additional insights. It allows applicants to provide a narrative that highlights specific accomplishments, addresses potential concerns, and explains career transitions.

Furthermore, cover letters enable candidates to explain any relevant information that might not be immediately evident from the resume, such as a passion for the industry or transferable skills from unrelated experiences. By complementing the resume, cover letters provide a holistic view of the applicant, facilitating a more comprehensive evaluation by potential employers.

In conclusion, cover letters remain a crucial component of the job application process. They offer applicants a unique opportunity to convey their qualifications, demonstrate motivation, showcase their personality, and complement their resume. In a competitive job market, a well-crafted cover letter can make a significant difference by capturing the attention of employers, setting applicants apart from their peers, and increasing their chances of securing an interview.

Therefore, job seekers should recognize the importance of investing time and effort into crafting compelling cover letters that effectively convey their suitability for the desired role and contribute to their overall success in the job application process.

Cover Letter Basics

Address your cover letter to the hiring manager—preferably by name.

The most common approach to address a cover letter is with the person's first and last name, followed by "Mr." or "Ms." (for example, "Dear Ms. Jane Doe" or simply "Dear Ms. Doe"). However, to avoid using the incorrect title or, worse, unknowingly misgendering someone, first and last name work just fine. Never use phrases like "To Whom It May Concern" or "Dear Sir or Madam."

Craft an opening paragraph that'll hook your reader.

Your introduction sets the tone for the rest of the cover letter. So you want it to be memorable, personable, conversational, and really relevant to the position you're applying for.

Make sure you indicate the job you're looking for (the hiring manager may be reviewing candidates for a half-dozen different positions). Yes, it's good to go with something simple like, "I am excited to apply for [job] with [Company]." Consider introducing yourself with a strong first paragraph showcasing your enthusiasm for the organization, your love for your work, and your previous accomplishments.

This is an excellent place to provide the "why" behind your application. Explain why you want this job at this company.

- In the opening paragraph, identify the position and capture the reader's attention.
- In the body of the letter, address any obvious questions; for example, if the job is located in another city, then state your willingness to relocate.
- In the closing paragraph, state your interest in the position and ask for an interview. Whatever you do, do not repeat your resume.
- And finally, proofread your Cover Letter. If need be, download Grammarly onto your computer so that you can double-check any potential errors.

Be sure to write a fresh cover letter for each job (but yes, you can use a template).

Utilizing the cover letter you wrote for your last application, making a small change to the company name, and sending it off is quicker and simpler. However, most employers prefer to see that you're really interested in each position and company, so drafting a different cover letter for each position is necessary.

While it's acceptable to reuse a few potent sentences and phrases from one cover letter to the next, don't even think about sending out a totally generic letter. The phrase "Dear Hiring Manager, I am excited to apply to the open position at your company" makes it plain to recruiters and hiring managers that you are mass-applying to all of the jobs listed on Indeed or LinkedIn.

Start by listing your contact info.

At the top of your cover letter, you should list your basic info. You can even copy the same heading from your resume if you'd like. Some contact info you might include (and the order you might include it) is:

- Your name
- Your location. List the city, but not the street address
- Your email address
- Your phone number (optional)
- Your LinkedIn, portfolio, or personal website URL (optional)

(Note that only name and email are mandatory, and you don't need to put a full address on a cover letter or resume anymore. A city and state (or metro area) are more than enough.)

Convey why you'd be a great hire for this job

A common cover letter blunder is merely mentioning how fantastic the position would be for you. Hiring managers are very aware of this; they really want to know <u>what you will add to the position and organization</u>. They also want to know how you will benefit the company.

After you've written your introduction, select a few key points that will form the body of your cover letter. They should demonstrate that you understand what the organization is looking for and explain how your background is relevant to the role. Look at the job description for hints. What issues does the organization hope to address with this hire? What abilities or experiences are discussed prominently or more than once? These are most likely the most critical requirements.

Choose three to five crucial qualifications that you believe best illustrate why you want this position at this company.

Back up your qualifications with examples and numbers

Examine your previous step's list of qualifications and think of examples from your past that demonstrate you have them. Also, look beyond your resume. Don't simply repeat what the recruiting manager can find elsewhere. You want to build a more complete picture of what experiences and accomplishments make you a fantastic hire and demonstrate what you can bring through their doors and deliver once hired.

Try asking yourself the following questions and finding responses that correspond to the qualifications you've decided to emphasize:

- How did you deal with one of the obligations listed in your resume?
- What information would you add if you were telling someone a (very brief!) story about how you achieved one of your resume bullet points?
- What aspect of your personality, passion, or work ethic makes you particularly adept at completing tasks?

Create your examples, then include some numbers. Hiring managers value statistics because they demonstrate that you have had a demonstrable impact on the organization for which you have worked. Did you bring in more clients than your competitors? Organize an astonishing amount of events? Make a work process 30% more efficient? Include it in your cover letter!

Finish with a strong conclusion.

It's tempting, according to the website muse.com, to take the last lines of your cover letter as a throwaway: "I look forward to hearing from you." However, your conclusion paragraph is your final opportunity to highlight your passion for the firm or how you'd be an excellent fit for the role. You can also utilize the end of your letter to include vital details, such as your willingness to relocate for the position.

Try this: "I believe my energy, desire to innovate, and experience as a sales leader will benefit The Northeast Widget Company greatly." I'd like to meet with you to explore the value I may bring as your next West Coast Sales Director. I appreciate your thoughtfulness and look forward to meeting with you soon."

Then, sign off professionally with a suitable closure and your first and last name.

Reread and revise.

Obviously, you should use spell-check on your cover letter, but keep in mind that having your computer search for mistakes isn't the same as editing. Set your letter aside for a day, or even just a few hours, and then reread it with fresh eyes—you'll almost certainly discover some adjustments you'd like to make. Don't be shy about downloading and using Grammarly.

You may even ask a friend or family member to look it over. You should ask them two questions in addition to asking if they see any errors:

1. Does this sell me as the best candidate for the job?
2. Does it pique your interest?

Return for another pass if the response to either is "no," or even a minor hesitation.

CHAPTER SIXTEEN

Overqualified? Should You "Dummy-Down" Your Resume?

"Today, many companies will not hire the candidates who are considered "Overqualified." However, ignoring the "overqualified" because you think they are too expensive, and you can hire two employees for the price of one, will eventually cost you in the long term. You can't Google experience.

— UNKNOWN.

Sometimes you will be overqualified for a job, but when you are in need of finding work, your current situation might warrant it. If you believe that you are overqualified for a particular job and are considering "dummying down" your resume, there are a few factors to consider before making a decision:

1. Job Requirements

Ensure that you fully understand the requirements and qualifications for the position. If you are genuinely overqualified and possess skills and experience that are not necessary for the role, it might be appropriate to tailor your resume to highlight the most relevant qualifications for that specific job.

2. Job market

Assess the current job market conditions and competition. If the market is highly competitive, showcasing your full qualifications might put you at a disadvantage, as employers may fear that you will quickly become dissatisfied or seek higher-level positions. In such cases, modifying your resume to match the job requirements more closely could increase your chances of being considered.

3. Career goals

Consider your long-term career goals. If taking a position that seems beneath your qualifications is a strategic move to enter a new industry or gain experience in a specific role, it might be worth emphasizing relevant skills and downplaying others. However, be careful not to misrepresent your qualifications or appear dishonest in the process.

4. Networking opportunities

Sometimes, applying for a position that appears lower-level can be a gateway to connecting with influential individuals in your desired industry. If you believe the job offers networking opportunities that align with your goals, it might be beneficial to apply with a modified resume.

5. Honest portrayal

It's essential to maintain honesty and integrity in your application materials. While you can emphasize certain qualifications over others, it is important not to falsify or misrepresent your skills or experience. Employers may verify your information during the hiring process, and being caught in a misrepresentation can harm your professional reputation.

Remember, there are alternative approaches to consider if you feel overqualified, such as explaining your motivations and desire for a particular position during an interview. Ultimately, the decision to "dummy down" your resume depends on your specific circumstances, the job market, and your long-term career goals.

CHAPTER SEVENTEEN

How to Ace an Interview: Key Strategies for Success

An interview is an important opportunity to demonstrate your abilities, experiences, and personality to potential employers. To perform well in an interview and maximize your chances of getting the job, you must prepare thoroughly and use efficient methods. From extensive research and confident body language to smart storytelling and deliberate follow-up, this chapter discusses the crucial techniques to help you master an interview. By following these rules, you will be able to portray yourself as the ideal applicant and leave an impact on the interviewers.

1. Research the Company and Position

Before the interview, conduct thorough research on the company and the position you are applying for. Familiarize yourself with the organization's mission, values, products/services, recent news, and competitors. This knowledge will demonstrate your genuine interest and dedication to the role. Additionally, learn about the specific job requirements, responsibilities, and qualifications. By understanding the company's needs, you can align your skills and experiences accordingly, making it easier to articulate how you can contribute to their success.

2. Prepare Your Responses

Anticipate common interview questions and prepare thoughtful responses in advance. Focus on showcasing your relevant experiences, accomplishments, and problem-solving abilities. Use the STAR method (Situation, Task, Action, Result) to structure your responses, providing specific examples that highlight your skills and achievements. Practice your answers to ensure clarity, conciseness, and coherence. Additionally, prepare questions to ask the interviewer to demonstrate your enthusiasm and curiosity about the position and the company.

3. Showcase Confidence and Professionalism

Confidence and professionalism are vital during an interview. Dress appropriately in professional attire, arrive on time, and maintain a positive attitude. Project confidence through your body language, such as maintaining eye contact, sitting upright, and using appropriate gestures. Speak clearly and with conviction, demonstrating your passion for the role. Active listening is equally important—show genuine interest in the interviewer's questions and comments, and respond thoughtfully. By projecting confidence and professionalism, you will leave a lasting impression and instill trust in the interviewer's mind.

4. Tell Compelling Stories

Craft compelling stories that illustrate your skills and experiences. Use specific examples to demonstrate how you have overcome challenges, achieved success, or collaborated effectively with others. Frame your stories in a concise and engaging manner, emphasizing the impact of your actions and highlighting the skills that align with the job requirements. By presenting memorable stories, you engage the interviewer, make your responses more memorable, and differentiate yourself from other candidates.

5. Follow-Up with a Thank-You Note

After the interview, send a personalized thank-you note to the interviewer(s). Express your appreciation for their time and reiterate your interest in the position. This gesture demonstrates your professionalism, attention to detail, and genuine enthusiasm for the opportunity. Customize each note to reflect the specific points discussed during the interview, reminding the interviewers of your qualifications and the positive impression you made. Such follow-up can set you apart from other candidates and leave a favorable impression.

Acing an interview requires careful preparation, confidence, and effective communication. By researching the company and position, preparing your responses, showcasing confidence and professionalism, telling compelling stories, and following up with a thank-you note, you can significantly enhance your chances of success and set yourself apart from other candidates Remember, each interview is a valuable learning experience that helps you refine your skills and grow as a professional. Good luck!

Hidden Secrets To Acing An Interview

Acing a job interview is a coveted skill that can significantly impact your career prospects. While there is no magic formula for success, understanding the key ingredients can give you a competitive edge. This section delves into the secret of acing a job interview by unraveling the essential elements that contribute to a successful outcome. From thorough preparation and confident communication to showcasing cultural fit and demonstrating a growth mindset, this section unveils the additional secrets to help you excel in your next job interview.

1. Showcasing Cultural Fit

Companies often prioritize cultural fit when assessing candidates. To ace an interview, research the company's culture, values, and work environment. Highlight your alignment with their values and demonstrate how you can contribute to their team dynamics. Share experiences that reflect your adaptability, collaboration skills, and ability to thrive in their work culture. Emphasize your understanding of the company's goals and show how your skills and personality align with their vision. By showcasing cultural fit, you increase your chances of being seen as a valuable addition to their team.

2. Demonstrating a Growth Mindset

Employers value candidates who exhibit a growth mindset—those who are open to learning, adaptable, and driven to improve. During the interview, discuss your willingness to embrace challenges, learn from failures, and continuously develop your skills. Highlight instances where you have taken the initiative sought feedback, and successfully overcome obstacles. Demonstrate your passion for professional growth and how it aligns with the company's goals. By showcasing a growth mindset, you position yourself as a motivated and proactive candidate.

Acing a job interview requires a combination of preparation, confident communication, showcasing cultural fit, and demonstrating a growth mindset. By investing time in thorough research, practicing your communication skills, aligning yourself with the company's culture, and exhibiting a willingness to learn and grow, you can increase your chances of success. Remember, every interview is an opportunity to learn and grow, regardless of the outcome. Embrace the process, leverage these secret ingredients, and strive for continuous improvement.

CHAPTER EIGHTEEN

An MBA Degree. Is It Worth It?

"More business decisions occur over lunch and dinner than at any other time, yet no MBA courses are given on the subject."

— PETER DRUCKER

My decision to pursue an MBA degree began in the late 1980s, we had only started to grow McLaughlin Enterprises, the research and development company we established after Pyxis. We focused on research into automotive and medical devices. One day, when my father and I were eating lunch together, he said, "You know, you should think about getting an MBA." This surprised me because it was a subject we had never talked about before.

I said, "Dad, I already have three degrees." One was a law degree so I was not interested in spending two more years working on an MBA

"Look," he said. You need an MBA to succeed in this business, according to David Holder (an investor) and a few other people I spoke with.

Previously, I was accepted into Seattle University's graduate school and contemplated earning an MBA there, but I ultimately decided to go back to Southern California and go to law school. Western State University College of Law and Pepperdine University both sent me acceptance letters. Ultimately, Western State had a night school program and offered more affordable tuition methods.

I continued to scoff at my dad's idea to go back to school to get an MBA Furthermore, it was costly and I couldn't afford to quit my job and return to school full-time. I simply did not have the time. At that time I was married and had three small children.

"Look, I'll make you a deal," my father said. Find a decent Executive Program, and I'll pay for it with company funds. At the very least, just consider it."

That night, I went home and told my wife about it. She, too, was concerned about the amount of time it would take. It was a lot of work having three children under the age of six and it didn't help that I traveled frequently for business. After a lengthy debate, she remarked, "I agree with your father." This is something I believe you should do. It can only benefit you an further your marketability."

I began to look into different Executive MBA programs at several local universities, albeit reluctantly. An acquaintance directed me to the Graduate Dean at Pepperdine's Graziadio School of Business. We had a fantastic meeting, and he explained the Presidential Key Executive Program (PKE) to me.

The PKE program was and continues to be a world-class, professionally and personally transformative Executive MBA program. It was created to put top-level executives in charge of corporate goal-setting, strategic decision-making, and bottom-line performance to the test. The PKE MBA is one level above an Executive MBA and the world's only program tailored for senior, C-suite executives and entrepreneurs. It provides a transformative experience that encourages critical thinking while also offering new and developing leadership trends and ideas.

Once a 20-month experience, it is now a 15-month experience in which professionals collaborate with colleagues from various industries to form a small cohort that serves as your personal advisory board. The goal is to challenge, encourage, and learn from one another, fostering an environment in which every leader is present at the table, forging lasting relationships, and broadening business perspectives.

My class featured a fantastic mix of high-level executives and entrepreneurs. We had an oil executive, one of the creators of Mrs. Fields Cookies, a senior officer from one of the nation's leading beer distributorships, numerous world-class engineers, and the future CEO of Power One. It was a fantastic group.

We'd meet once a month at the corporate offices of one of the cohort's companies. We'd meet all day Friday and Saturday. It took a lot of planning and traveling.

Was it, in my perspective, worthwhile? Absolutely. It took a lot of work, and I spent a lot of time away from my family, but it was well worth it. The amount of labor and the difficulty of the work startled me, but I worked harder for my MBA than I did for any other degree. It is also the most important to me. The personal experiences, engagement, and insight were priceless.

I was also extremely fortunate and grateful to have my family's business pay for it.

The Master of Business Administration (MBA) has long been considered a prestigious degree that can offer substantial value and career advancement. However, in recent years, there has been a concerning decline in the MBA's 'value added ratio,' which refers to the degree's ability to provide a significant return on investment in terms of knowledge, skills, and career prospects.

Let's look at the factors contributing to this decline, including market saturation, changing business landscapes, and the rise of alternative education and skill development avenues. It also examines potential solutions to restore the MBA's value and relevance in today's professional world.

1. Market Saturation and Degree Inflation

According to AACSB.edu, the proliferation of MBA programs and graduates has led to market saturation, resulting in an oversupply of degree holders. With more professionals possessing an MBA, the degree's perceived value has diminished, making it harder for graduates to differentiate themselves in a crowded job market. Employers may question the actual value and unique skills offered by an MBA, contributing to the decline in the degree's 'value added ratio.'

2. Changing Business Landscapes and Skill Demands

The usefulness of conventional MBA courses has been challenged by the dynamic nature of business landscapes, which are characterized by quick technical breakthroughs, globalization, and fluctuating industry demands. Employers are looking for employees with particular talents in fields like entrepreneurship, digital marketing, and data analysis. These changing skill requirements may not be effectively matched by the standard MBA curriculum, which is frequently generic and focuses on broad business principles, which lowers the perceived value of the degree.

3. Rise of Alternative Education and Skill Development

Alternative education and skill development avenues, such as online courses, boot camps, and industry-specific certifications, have gained popularity as they offer targeted and practical knowledge. These alternatives often provide more focused and immediately applicable skills compared to the broader knowledge acquired through an MBA. As professionals seek faster and more cost-effective ways to upskill and pivot careers, these alternatives challenge the MBA's value proposition.

4. Adaptation of MBA Programs

Institutions that provide MBA programs have started to adapt to the changing needs of students and businesses. MBA schools may make sure that their graduates have the abilities and information that employers are looking for by including specialized tracks, modernized curricula, and opportunities for experiential learning. Internships, real-world initiatives, and collaboration with business partners can improve practical applicability and relevance. Research into the different programs and curricula that the different programs offer will ensure a good fit.

The Cost Factor

The skyrocketing cost of college tuition today poses significant challenges for aspiring MBA business students. The increasing tuition fees, associated expenses, and opportunity cost of leaving the workforce create financial barriers and question the return on investment.

Many universities now provide detailed information on the cost breakdown of the program, including tuition, fees, and other expenses presenting clear and comprehensive information allows students to make informed decisions to plan their finances accordingly.

By offering flexible program structures students are provided with options to customize their MBA experience based on their career goals and financial constraints. This could include part-time or accelerated programs, allowing students to continue working while pursuing their degree or completing the program in a shorter timeframe.

Some universities encourage employer sponsorship for MBA programs which can significantly reduce the financial burden on students. Universities have established partnerships with corporations to provide financial support, scholarships, or tuition reimbursement programs for their employees pursuing an MBA.

There are also income share agreements (ISAs) which are financial arrangements where students agree to pay a percentage of their future income for a specified period after graduation instead of paying tuition fees. Implementing ISAs can help students manage the immediate financial burden and align their payments with their income levels.

One may also explore alternative financing options, such as low-interest loans, crowdfunding platforms, or peer-to-peer lending, which can provide students with additional avenues to fund their MBA education. Universities sometime collaborate with financial institutions to offer specialized loan programs tailored to MBA students.

Programs that leverage open educational resources (OER), such as free or low-cost textbooks, online course materials, and educational platforms, can also help reduce the expenses associated with the costs.

It has become necessary for universities to prioritize affordability while maintaining the quality and value of the MBA program. Implementing a combination of these strategies, tailored to the specific context and needs of the institution. Doing your research can help alleviate the excessive cost and financial burden of pursuing an MBA.

The supply and demand within your specific career path

The supply and demand status for MBA students today can vary depending on factors such as location, program reputation, specialization, and industry trends. Here are some key points to consider:

Supply:

1. Increasing Number of MBA Programs

Over the years, the number of MBA programs globally has expanded, leading to a greater supply of MBA graduates. Many universities and business schools now offer MBA programs to meet the demand for advanced business education.

2. Market Saturation

The increase in the number of MBA programs has resulted in market saturation, particularly in certain regions and industries. This means that there may be a higher number of MBA graduates competing for limited job opportunities.

Demand:

1. Industry Relevance

The demand for MBA graduates varies across industries. Traditionally, sectors such as consulting, finance, and technology have shown high demand for MBA talent. However, the demand may fluctuate based on economic conditions, industry trends, and emerging fields such as data analytics, entrepreneurship, and sustainable business.

2. Specializations and Skills

The demand for MBA graduates with specific specializations or skills can differ. Employers often seek candidates with expertise in areas such as finance, marketing, strategy, operations, or leadership, depending on their organizational needs.

3. Global Opportunities

The demand for MBA graduates is not limited to a specific geographical region. The globalization of business has created opportunities for MBA students to work in various countries and industries, expanding their career prospects.

It is important to note that while the demand for MBA graduates remains strong in certain sectors, the value placed on an MBA degree has evolved. Employers increasingly seek candidates with a combination of business acumen, practical skills, and relevant experience.

Many Companies may also consider alternative educational paths and professional certifications alongside or in lieu of an MBA.

Overall, while the demand for MBA graduates continues to exist, it is essential for individuals pursuing an MBA to carefully consider their career goals, and market trends, and align their skill set with industry needs to maximize their opportunities for success.

Here are a few factors to consider when assessing whether pursuing an MBA aligns with your goals and circumstances:

1. Career Goals

Evaluate your career goals and determine if an MBA will contribute to your desired professional trajectory. Consider how the knowledge, skills, and networks gained from an MBA program can enhance your career opportunities and advancement.

2. Relevance and Fit

Assess the relevance of an MBA to your current or desired field. Research the program's curriculum, specializations, and career outcomes to ensure it aligns with your specific interests and goals.

3. Experience and Perspective

Your work experience can bring valuable insights and perspectives to the MBA classroom. You can leverage your professional background to contribute to class discussions and enrich your learning experience.

4. Networking Opportunities

Consider the networking opportunities an MBA program can provide, both with classmates and alumni. Networking can be valuable at any age and can open doors to new connections, mentorship, and career opportunities.

5. Flexibility of Program Formats

Explore various MBA program formats, such as full-time, part-time, or executive MBA programs. Some formats are specifically designed for working professionals, allowing you to balance your work commitments while pursuing your degree.

6. Personal Readiness

Assess your personal readiness to commit to the demands of an MBA program, including the time and financial investment required. Consider your personal and family responsibilities and ensure you can balance these with the demands of the program.

Ultimately, the decision to pursue an MBA should be based on a careful evaluation of your goals, circumstances, and commitment. Again, do your research, **Age should not be a deterrent**. If you believe that an MBA will provide value and contribute to your long-term professional growth and fulfillment.

What is an Executive MBA?

Executive MBAs are more streamlined than traditional MBA programs, though there is substantial overlap in their curricula and objectives. They have more stringent entry requirements and prepare graduates for more advanced career opportunities, frequently at the executive level.

The average Executive MBA student is 38, or about ten years older than the average MBA student. They also have over a decade of work experience, often in a managerial role.

Why get an Executive MBA?

This is an excellent degree for experienced professionals seriously trying to become executives. These programs promote networking and career development opportunities. At top programs, you'll have the opportunity to connect with classmates who may be directors or vice presidents of companies.

How much does an Executive MBA cost?

The price tag for a top program can easily surpass $200,000, similar to the best traditional MBA programs. The average cost of an EMBA is closer to $80,000.

Networking Opportunities: EMBA vs. MBA

This is one of the main areas where EMBA programs often provide greater value than a traditional MBA. EMBAs frequently put students into cohorts, allowing students to develop connections with classmates who hold high-ranking positions. They also offer networking events, guest lectures, career resources, and access to recruiters.

Traditional MBA programs are also good for networking; by offering many of the same opportunities. EMBA programs simply do it all on a higher level—partly because students are further in their careers.

Alumni connections EMBA vs. MBA

Utilizing alumni connections can be an excellent form of networking. Schools with strong alumni networks help graduates land great jobs faster than others. Alumni connections are useful at every education level, but EMBA students typically realize greater benefits than, say, someone with a bachelor's degree.

Executive MBA applications and admissions

EMBA programs accept a greater percentage of applicants than traditional full-time MBA programs. For top schools, such as the University of Michigan and the University of Pennsylvania, the difference in acceptance rate can be over 50 percent, according to *Poets and Quants*.

Executive MBA salary

Most incoming EMBA students are already earning six figures when they start a program, but having an EMBA from a top school could potentially double your earnings.

Will business schools accept your application if you're an older candidate?

Schools are also aware that recruiters at top firms like McKinsey or Goldman Sachs prefer to hire young associates and analysts into their graduate programs, as they're easier to mold and are likely to have fewer family commitments. But business schools also champion diversity, and most want a wide range of people in their cohorts, which may help your application.

"They want students to have interesting experiences to share in classroom discussions," explains David White, MBA admissions consultant and founding partner of Menlo Coaching.

So, your experience could be played to your advantage. You've probably had the chance to work on a big project or had an impressive achievement during your career, which you can leverage to boost your application. As with anybody applying to business school, it's about communicating that you're a good fit.

For Those of You Who Are Still Unsure

A standard full-time MBA can be finished in around two years. It is challenging to work and study at the same time because of the curriculum and course load. Part-time MBA programs might appear more convenient if you want to keep your employment while pursuing your degree, but they can take three to five years to complete.

MBA programs are designed to train the next generation of corporate executives, but the degree itself doesn't guarantee that you will achieve a high-paying job or a leadership position. In fact, there are over 200,000 MBA graduates each year, making an MBA a frequent feature on a resume. Your decision to go for this degree will be customized for you and your personal circumstances.

CHAPTER NINETEEN

Age Discrimination in the Business World

Ageism is as odious as racism and sexism.

— CLAUDE PEPPER

As an older executive, there have been times when I have been in the middle of a job interview and you got the feeling that the company I was interviewing with had no intention of hiring me. The expressions on their faces can be very telling. What you see is a mixture of sympathy and scorn. Imagine that you are around 45-50 years old and they think you're too old for the position. This is something that happens all the time. Ageism is a more frequent term for age discrimination.

Pyxis along with our second family startup, TPMS (Tire Pressure Monitoring System), the company we started to create a tire pressure monitoring system, were two pretty significant "home runs" for me in the business world, so I assumed getting a job at the C-level would be simple. I underestimated how difficult it would be.

I've always taken good care of myself, so I always appeared younger than I was. However, taking care of myself, keeping my mind fresh, and developing the other abilities required to run a business was of little or no use as I encountered a lot of rejection for the first time in my life. The majority of the jobs I had sought out when I was younger seemed simple to land. Perhaps it spoiled me, but it was a completely new experience for me to enter the job market as a C-level executive and be met with age discrimination.

Apparently, this isn't a new phenomenon because, in 1967, the Age Discrimination in Employment Act (ADEA) was enacted. Age has been one of the "protected characteristics" in the workplace since that time, which implies that companies cannot discriminate against employees based on their age. Hiring, firing, work assignments, and promotions are all examples of this. This legal protection does not apply to employees of smaller enterprises because businesses with less than 20 employees are exempt from the ADEA.

Older folks in the workplace are oftentimes being gently urged out the door. It may appear that others are not taking you as seriously as they once did. Maybe you are excluded from meetings. You might feel like you are being interrogated. Your point of view is being overlooked.

There is a subtle tension in which older individuals are expected to stand aside, get out of the way, and stop creating a perceived bottleneck in the distribution of resources, jobs, or positions of influence so that the younger generation can have their turn.

Ageism is so socially acceptable that it's not uncommon for people to dismiss it as a bias. Age discrimination is also becoming increasingly difficult to prove.

One of the most common misconceptions about recruiting older workers is that they command higher salaries based on their experience and they don't perform as well as younger people. And I'm sure that might happen in some situations, sectors, or roles. However, according to statistics, job performance does not deteriorate with age.

So, what should you do if you feel you are a victim of Ageism in the workplace?

To begin with, don't believe that you or your workplace are completely immune to age discrimination. For speedier processing and decision-making, our brains rely on established stereotypes. Recognize your own thought patterns. Examine your preconceptions. If you notice indicators of Ageism that aren't directed at you, don't dismiss them by reasoning that it could never happen to you.

If this has been your experience, here's how to cope with workplace ageism:

1. Invest in your ongoing development and growth. Read, remain current on trends and best practices, and strive to do better each year. Find a mentor, either within or outside of your current firm, who is committed to your growth.

2. Commit to combating the notion of an elderly professional who is resistant to change and technology, has little energy, and coasts without ambition. The older generation today possesses a plethora of industry and institutional knowledge. Don't believe that your company "owes you" anything for your previous contributions.
3. Exhibit the same polish and professionalism as your younger coworkers. Don't put too much stock in your status as an established contributor. Don't be afraid to go above and beyond to represent your organization.
4. Finally, if you encounter indicators of age discrimination, make thorough notes, including the dates and names of witnesses to conversations. Contact an employment lawyer who can evaluate your position and advise you on the next measures.

Maintain an active network and keep your alternatives open, just like your younger colleagues. Spend some time each year revising your resume and online profiles; make sure to follow the most recent standards to avoid looking out of date. At the end of the day, the greatest approach to avoid being subjected to age discrimination is to stay on top of your career.

CHAPTER TWENTY
Take a Look in the Mirror

Imagine you've lost your job, your industry is collapsing, and you need to reinvent yourself. Whether you are young or older you will have to make some big decisions and the road ahead will be difficult at times. The topics we'll cover here are uncomfortable by today's standards, but the reality is that you have to accept the situation for what it is. Over the years, I've learned that there are occasions when you need to take a long, hard look in the mirror.

Early in my career, I got the opportunity to meet Squire Fridell who is an American retired actor and author best known for his work in over 3,000 television advertisements; he also played Ronald McDonald in McDonald's commercials from 1985 to 1991. I met Squire during a book signing for his book, Acting in Television Commercials for Fun and Profit.

He noted in his book, "If you don't like what you see in the mirror, you need to make a change." This notion has resonated with me for decades and is more pertinent today than ever.

I'm not talking about big modifications like plastic surgery. I'm talking about the minor details. Are you physically fit? Do you need to implement a healthier lifestyle? Update your hairstyle? Change some aspect of your personality? Why should this matter? Because, like it or not, in the business world, it does matter.

Your Body Mass Index

Being overweight or even obese, is now accepted in our society, thanks to our society's tolerance and sensitivity.

But truthfully, being overweight not only is bad for your health but can have an impact on your prospects of employment. Maybe it's time to work on creating a healthier lifestyle. This may vary based on a variety of factors such as the industry, the exact job requirements, and the biases of employers or hiring managers. Weight discrimination in the workplace is widely regarded as immoral and, in many areas, illegal. However, even if weight bias is not openly acknowledged, it can still exist and impact hiring decisions.

Obesity rates in the United States are rising. Obesity will affect 113 million Americans by the end of 2023. According to a recent analysis by GlobalData researchers, the United States had the most overweight people by the end of 2022. Other findings from the survey suggest that obesity affects women more than males in the United States. According to the most recent American Heart Association (AHA) figures, 60-70% of the U.S. population is overweight or obese.

Here are a few ways in which being overweight may potentially affect employment opportunities:

1. Perceived Physical Capabilities

Some job roles, such as physically demanding jobs or those requiring specific physical standards, may have certain weight or fitness requirements. If an employer perceives that an overweight candidate may not meet these requirements, they might choose someone else who they believe is more physically fit.

2. Appearance and Professional Image

In certain industries where physical appearance is considered essential, such as modeling or customer-facing roles, some employers may hold biases against overweight individuals, believing that their appearance doesn't align with the company's image or the expectations of their customers.

3. Stereotypes and Biases

Unconscious biases can exist, leading to assumptions about a person's work ethic, discipline, or health based solely on their weight. These biases may result in unfair judgments about a candidate's qualifications or abilities.

4. Health Insurance Costs

In countries where employers provide health insurance coverage, overweight individuals may be associated with potentially higher healthcare costs. Some employers might take this into consideration when making hiring decisions to manage their healthcare expenses.

It's important to recognize that these potential biases and discrimination are unfair and discriminatory practices. Many organizations have policies in place to prevent such discrimination and promote diversity and inclusion. Laws also exist in some jurisdictions to protect individuals from weight-based discrimination. If you believe you have been discriminated against due to your weight during the hiring process or during employment, you may want to consult with a legal professional or a relevant employment rights organization to understand your rights and options. But understand, wrong as it may be, your appearance does matter in the business world.

New Hairstyle or Perhaps Color Your Gray Hair?

There is silvery white hair, and then again, there is dull gray hair. This has been an ongoing question for men and women for decades. Do I stay gray, or do I add a little color?

The acceptability of a man or a woman coloring their hair to look younger in the business world can vary depending on cultural norms, industry standards, and individual company policies. In general, personal appearance and grooming play a role in professional settings.

In many modern workplaces, there is an increasing emphasis on diversity, inclusivity, and acceptance of individual expression. As a result, there is often more flexibility in terms of personal appearance, including hair color. Many companies prioritize a candidate's skills, qualifications, and performance over physical attributes such as hair color.

However, it's important to note that there may still be some industries or specific organizations that have more conservative expectations regarding personal appearance, including hair color. In such cases, natural hair colors may be preferred or expected.

If you perceive age as a barrier to getting a job and you believe that coloring your hair might help counteract that perception, it could be an option to consider. Coloring your hair to appear younger is a personal choice that some individuals make to enhance their self-confidence and potentially mitigate age-related biases. Ultimately, being clean and well-groomed could be the difference in landing a job or not.

Here are a few points to consider when contemplating any changes to your appearance as it relates to your job search.

1. Industry and Company Culture

Research the industry and specific companies you're interested in to understand their culture and expectations regarding personal appearance. Some industries, such as creative fields or tech startups, may embrace individual expression and be more accepting of unconventional hair colors. In contrast, other industries, like finance or law, may have more conservative expectations.

2. Balance Professionalism

While you may wish to appear younger, it's important to maintain a professional image. Choose a hair color that complements your overall appearance and aligns with the professional norms of your industry.

3. Skills and Experience

Remember that your skills, experience, and qualifications are crucial factors in securing a job. While altering your appearance may help initially, focusing on highlighting your expertise and demonstrating your value as a candidate will be the most significant contributor to long-term success.

4. Confidence and Authenticity

Confidence is key during the job search process. If coloring your hair gives you an added sense of self-assurance, it may positively impact your overall demeanor and performance in interviews. However, it's essential to remain authentic and true to yourself throughout the process.

Beards and Facial Hair.

The impact of beards or facial hair on employment in the business world can vary depending on various factors, including industry norms, company culture, and individual preferences of employers or hiring managers. Here are a few considerations:

1. Industry and Company Culture

Different industries have different expectations regarding personal appearance. Some industries, such as creative fields or tech startups, may be more accepting of beards and facial hair as they prioritize individual expression. On the other hand, more conservative industries like finance or law may have stricter grooming standards that require a clean-shaven look or well-groomed facial hair.

2. Professionalism and Cleanliness

In any industry, it's generally important to maintain a professional and well-groomed appearance. If you choose to have a beard or facial hair, ensure that it is well-maintained, neatly trimmed, and clean. A well-groomed beard or facial hair is less likely to be a hindrance to employment compared to an unkempt or messy appearance.

3. Company Policies and Preferences

Some companies may have specific policies or guidelines regarding grooming and appearance, including rules about beards or facial hair. It's essential to research the company's policies and consider them when deciding how to present yourself during the hiring process.

4. First Impressions and Prejudices

It's important to acknowledge that biases and prejudices can exist, even if they are unconscious or unintentional. Some employers or hiring managers may have personal preferences or stereotypes associated with beards or facial hair. While it may not be fair, it could potentially influence their perception of a candidate. However, many employers prioritize skills, qualifications, and experience over physical appearance.

Ultimately, it's advisable to research and consider the industry norms, specific company culture, and grooming expectations when deciding whether to have a beard or facial hair. While there may be some biases or preferences, there are also many successful professionals who maintain beards or facial hair. It's important to present yourself confidently, professionally, and in a manner that aligns with your industry and the organization you're applying to.

Men: Make sure you trim your nostril hair, ear hair, and eyebrows. You don't want to walk into the interview looking like Rasputin, the mad monk.

Women: Choose your make-up wisely, too much or none at all, could the difference in the way the interviewer perceives you.

Men: The Importance of the Suit You Wear on a Job Interview

In today's competitive job market, making a positive first impression during a job interview is crucial. While qualifications, skills, and experience play a significant role, the impact of one's appearance should not be underestimated. Among the many elements that contribute to a polished and professional image, the suit you choose to wear holds great significance. This section explores the importance of the suit you wear during a job interview, highlighting its role in conveying professionalism, confidence, and respect for the opportunity.

1. Symbol of Professionalism

For men, a well-tailored suit is a symbol of professionalism and is often associated with traditional business attire. By donning a suit, you demonstrate your understanding of the importance of presenting yourself in a manner appropriate for professional settings. It sends a clear message to potential employers that you take the job opportunity seriously and are committed to projecting a polished and competent image.

2. Creates a Positive First Impression

First impressions are formed within seconds of meeting someone, and the clothing you wear greatly influences this initial perception. It exudes professionalism, attention to detail, and a level of sophistication. It conveys that you have made an effort to present yourself in the best possible manner, capturing the attention and respect of interviewers from the moment you enter the room.

3. Boosts Confidence

Wearing a well-fitted suit can significantly boost your confidence during a job interview. When you are dressed in attire that makes you feel comfortable and self-assured, it positively impacts your overall demeanor. Confidence is an essential trait that interviewers look for in candidates as it suggests an ability to handle challenges, communicate effectively, and make sound decisions. A suit, therefore, serves as a psychological tool that empowers you to perform at your best.

4. Reflects Attention to Detail

The clothing you choose to wear reflects your attention to detail, a characteristic that is highly valued in many professional environments. A well-coordinated ensemble, paired with appropriate accessories and grooming, demonstrates your ability to pay attention to the finer points. Employers often perceive individuals who display attention to detail in their appearance as likely to exhibit the same level of meticulousness in their work.

5. Adaptable to Various Work Environments

A suit is a versatile garment that can be adapted to suit various work environments, including formal, semi-formal, and professional settings. It allows you to project a polished image regardless of the specific company culture or industry norms. Whether you are interviewing for a corporate position or a creative role, a suit can be adjusted through color, pattern, and accessories to align with the expectations of the respective workplace.

In conclusion, the suit you wear on a job interview holds significant importance as it communicates professionalism, creates a positive first impression, boosts confidence, reflects attention to detail, and is adaptable to various work environments.

While the suit alone cannot guarantee success in securing a job, it plays a pivotal role in setting the tone for the interview and positioning yourself as a serious and capable candidate. Investing time and effort into selecting and maintaining an appropriate suit demonstrates your commitment to professional excellence and greatly enhances your chances of success in today's competitive job market.

When it comes to suits, wear blue, not gray. Gray gives off an older vibe. Blue is always safe. The only exception to this is for the very young. They can get away with wearing gray. I recommend that the suit be dark. The shirt should be a solid color—white, yellow, or light blue. Also, ensure the formal shirt you are wearing is ironed or pressed. Nothing looks worse than a wrinkled shirt underneath a sharp suit. Do not wear a black shirt. This isn't a casting call for a remake of The Sopranos.

The ties should be solid or with a subtle stripe: no Tommy Bahama ties or a tie from Dick's Last Resort.

You should wear shoes that CAN BE POLISHED. Either black or brown. No suede, desert boots, or sneakers.

Women: The Importance of the Outfit a Woman Wears to a Job Interview

In today's professional landscape, women face unique challenges when it comes to making a positive first impression during a job interview. While qualifications, skills, and experience remain essential, the outfit a woman chooses to wear holds great significance. This section explores the importance of the outfit a woman wears to a job interview, highlighting its role in conveying professionalism, confidence, and personal branding.

1. Professionalism and Industry Expectations

Selecting an outfit that aligns with professional standards and the expectations of the industry is crucial. Different fields have varying dress codes, ranging from formal to business casual. By dressing appropriately, a woman demonstrates her understanding of the professional environment she seeks to join. This attention to detail conveys a level of professionalism that can positively influence the interviewer's perception of her suitability for the position.

2. Building a Positive First Impression

First impressions are formed quickly and can significantly impact the interview process. The outfit a woman wears plays a key role in creating a positive initial perception. A well-chosen and well-fitted outfit signals that she has taken the time and effort to present herself in the best possible manner. It conveys professionalism, attention to detail, and a respect for the opportunity. A polished appearance can capture the attention and respect of interviewers from the moment she enters the room.

3. Reflecting Personal Branding

An outfit serves as a medium for personal branding, allowing a woman to communicate her unique qualities and professional identity. By carefully selecting attire that represents her style, values, and industry knowledge, she can create a cohesive and authentic personal brand. This consistent representation across her outfit, resume, and interview responses reinforces her suitability for the role and helps her stand out among other candidates.

4. Boosting Confidence

Wearing an outfit that makes a woman feel confident can have a significant impact on her performance during a job interview. When she is dressed in attire that aligns with her personal style and makes her feel comfortable, she exudes confidence and self-assurance. This confidence translates into better body language, improved communication, and an overall more positive demeanor, which can greatly influence the interviewer's perception of her capabilities.

5. Non-Verbal Communication and Attention to Detail

The outfit a woman wears reflects her attention to detail and non-verbal communication skills, both of which are highly valued in professional environments. From the choice of clothing to the coordination of accessories and grooming, attention to detail demonstrates her ability to present herself in a polished and well-prepared manner. These qualities suggest that she is likely to exhibit the same level of meticulousness in her work.

In conclusion, the outfit a woman wears to a job interview holds immense importance in conveying professionalism, creating a positive first impression, reflecting personal branding, boosting confidence, and demonstrating attention to detail.

By carefully selecting an appropriate and well-fitted outfit, a woman can align herself with industry expectations, project confidence, and effectively communicate her personal brand.

While attire alone does not determine success, it significantly influences how she is perceived and positions her as a serious and capable candidate. Investing time and effort into selecting an appropriate outfit demonstrates her commitment to professional excellence and greatly enhances her chances of success in today's competitive job market.

Here are the fundamentals of what women should wear to a professional interview:

- A suit in navy, black, or dark gray
- Suit skirt just below or above the knee
- Coordinated blouse
- Conservative shoes
- Limited jewelry
- No huge dangling earrings or arms full of bracelets
- No jewelry is better than cheap jewelry

- Professional hairstyle
- Neutral-colored pantyhose
- Light makeup and a limited amount of perfume
- Clean, neatly manicured nails
- Have a professional bag or briefcase.

If You Wear Glasses

If you wear glasses, you might want to rethink them. Glasses can indicate you are getting older, and your eyes aren't that good anymore. If you are very young, they are okay. If you are in the process of recreating yourself, try contact lenses. Particularly if you are changing careers and hunting for a new job. Does this sound a little harsh? Yes, it does. But it's what you should do.

I had worn glasses since the age of six. Sometimes, they were a massive pain in the rear, but I survived and thrived. When I got out of college, I finally got contact lenses. They were great for sports and other activities, but I always found them uncomfortable. It always felt like I had a speck of sand in each eye. Twenty years ago, I opted for Lasik, and it was one of the smartest decisions I ever made. In one day, I disposed of over $2000 worth of prescription sunglasses and regular glasses. Lasik is not cheap. On average, Lasik surgery costs $1500 to $3000 per eye. For me, it was a godsend. Do I think it's worth it? Yes. Especially if you are recreating yourself.

Adjusting Your Personality Traits

Introverts:

- If you are introverted, your ability to succeed in a job interview shouldn't be hampered by your shyness and introversion. Numerous eminent professionals have introverted personalities, and you may succeed in interviews too with sufficient practice and planning.

Here are some pointers to make an impression at a job interview:

- Make sure you adequately prepare. Do your homework on the business, the position you're applying for, and the sector. You'll feel more assured throughout the interview the more you understand the company and its ideals.
- Prepare responses to frequently asked interview questions and run them by a friend or out loud. You'll be able to express your ideas more effectively and become more confident as a result.
- People that are introverted frequently have valuable qualities including keen listening abilities, attention to detail, and thinking. During the interview, highlight these qualities and demonstrate how they help you contribute to the firm.
- Ask a friend or relative to act as the interviewer while you conduct a practice interview. This can help you gain confidence and practice answering questions under time constraints.
- Create a succinct overview of your qualifications for the position, your experience, and your talents. This might assist you in making a confident introduction at the start of the interview.
- Utilize your listening abilities. Actively participate in the interview by paying attention to the interviewer's queries. Before responding, pause to collect your thoughts. Make sure your replies directly address the question.
- Prepare a list of inquiries to make to the interviewer. This shows that you are interested in the business and the position, and it also gives you a chance to learn more about the corporate culture.

- Don't rush through the interview; take your time. It's acceptable to pause and consider a question before responding. Don't feel compelled to immediately fill silences; instead, speak clearly and gently.
- Be sure to exercise good body language. Maintain eye contact with the interviewer (or at the very least, glance at their chin or forehead) and take care of your posture. Even if you feel a little uneasy, confident body language can project self-assurance.

You can use your introversion to your advantage. Although introverts may dislike small talk and overly sociable situations, they frequently thrive at developing more meaningful relationships and demonstrating empathy. In order to foster excellent team relationships, emphasize these qualities.

Gain as much experience as you can in interviews. Consider submitting applications for positions that may not initially be your top choices in order to obtain more interview practice. The more interviews you have, the more at ease and assured you'll feel.

Keep in mind that interviewers are aware that each person has a unique personality. Being quiet and reserved doesn't preclude you from being competent or prepared for the position. Making a strong impression on the interviewer by demonstrating your abilities, experience, and enthusiasm for the position. During the interview process, just be yourself and let your individuality shine.

Renew your effort.

Extroverted.

- If you are extroverted and you have a tendency to ramble on too long during interviews, it's important to strike a balance between highlighting your skills and experiences while also remaining succinct and on-topic.

Here are a few more pointers to help you ace your job interview:

- Listen attentively. Make an attempt to pay close attention to the interviewer's inquiries. Before responding, take time to comprehend what they are asking. This will enable you to give more pertinent and focused responses.
- Ensure that you plan beforehand. Prepare your answers to typical interview questions in advance. You can prevent rambling or going off on tangents by having prepared responses.
- When answering questions, be concise. Without going into great detail, cover the essentials. After providing a succinct response, you can always inquire as to whether the interviewer would like more details or instances.
- Apply the STAR approach. Use the STAR approach (Situation, Task, Action, Result) to organize your responses when discussing specific experiences or circumstances. With the use of this technique, you may better structure your response and avoid talking too much.
- Practice answering questions in a limited amount of time. During practice interviews, you can record yourself or ask a buddy to time you. You can use this practice to increase your awareness of how much you talk as well as your time management abilities.
- When you've finished addressing a question, pause for a moment to determine whether you've done it sufficiently. This can assist you prevent subsequently adding extra information.

If you're unsure of your interviewing approach, try considering getting input from close friends, family members, or a professional counselor. They can offer perceptions and recommendations on how to enhance your interview communication.

Make sure to prepare thoughtful questions for the interviewer rather than utilizing all of your talking time to respond to their queries. This gives you the opportunity to learn more about the position while also demonstrating your interest in the role and organization.

During the interview, be aware of your propensity for talking excessively. Gently guide yourself back to the primary idea if you find yourself straying from the subject or giving too many details.

Keep your eyes fixed on the interviewer to practice active listening. You may use this to determine how interested they are and modify your responses accordingly.

To succeed in an interview, keep in mind that you must successfully convey your qualifications, experiences, and enthusiasm for the position. To leave a good impression on the interviewer, concentrate on answering each question with clarity, concision, and relevance.

Final Thoughts

Although your credentials, abilities, and experience are unquestionably key considerations in the employment process, how a potential employer perceives you could be greatly influenced by your initial impression.

Being clean, well-groomed, and in good physical shape, can give you an advantage, but it's vital to remember that this is only one part of the total package. It won't make up for a resume that is badly written, lacks experience or abilities, or both. During the job application process, it's critical to combine a polished appearance with a solid skill set and the ability to clearly communicate your qualifications.

It's a little investment that, in the cutthroat job market, can generate significant rewards.

CHAPTER TWENTY-ONE
Networking

You can make more friends in two months by becoming interested in other people than you can in two years by trying to get other people interested in you.

— DALE CARNEGIE

Assume you are a bit shy and despise networking. Here's why you should shift your perspective.

Networking isn't always at the top of everyone's priority list. It can be time-consuming, embarrassing at times, and extremely draining. When your schedule is already jam-packed with work and family obligations, the last thing you want to do is make small talk with strangers.

However, there is no doubting the influence a strong professional network may have on your professional success. When done correctly, networking will not only help you obtain a job faster, but it will also provide you with a competitive advantage throughout your career. Let's discuss what you can do to improve your networking skills as your career progresses.

What is networking?

Networking isn't merely the exchange of information with others. Networking is about establishing, building, and nurturing long-term, mutually beneficial relationships with the people you meet, whether you're waiting to order your morning coffee, participating in a sports league, or attending a work conference. You don't have to join a number of professional associations and attend every networking event that comes your way in order to be a successful networker. In fact, if you take your eyes off your smartphone when you're out in public, you'll see that networking opportunities are all around you every day.

The Importance of Networking in the Business World

In today's fast-paced and interconnected business landscape, networking has emerged as a vital tool for professional success.

While technical skills and expertise are undoubtedly valuable, the ability to build and maintain meaningful connections with others is equally essential. Let's explore the importance of networking in the business world, highlighting its role in fostering opportunities, knowledge sharing, professional growth, and personal development. It's also an indispensable tool for recreating yourself.

1. Creating Opportunities.

Networking opens doors to numerous opportunities that may not be readily available through traditional means. Building relationships with professionals, industry leaders, and potential mentors allows you to tap into the hidden job market, gain access to unadvertised positions, and discover new business ventures or collaborations. Networking expands your sphere of influence and increases the likelihood of being in the right place at the right time to seize promising opportunities.

2. Knowledge Sharing and Learning.

Networking provides a platform for knowledge sharing and learning from others' experiences. Engaging with professionals from diverse backgrounds and industries offers fresh perspectives, insights, and innovative ideas. Through conversations and discussions, people can exchange best practices, learn about emerging trends, and stay updated on industry developments. This valuable knowledge can contribute to personal and professional growth, enhancing problem-solving abilities and fostering creativity.

3. Building a Supportive Community.

Networking creates a supportive community of like-minded professionals who can provide guidance, advice, and mentorship. These relationships can offer a sounding board for ideas, constructive feedback, and encouragement during challenging times. The business world can be competitive and demanding, but a strong network provides a sense of camaraderie and a support system that can help navigate obstacles and promote overall well-being.

4. Access to Resources and Expertise.

Networking allows you to tap into a vast pool of resources and expertise. Connections made through networking can provide access to specialized knowledge, industry-specific insights, and valuable contacts. Whether seeking advice on a complex project, guidance on career advancement, or access to funding for a new venture, a robust network offers a wealth of resources that can accelerate professional growth and success.

5. Enhancing Visibility and Building a Personal Brand.

Networking enables you to enhance your visibility within their industry or professional community. Active participation in industry events, conferences, and online platforms allows you to establish a strong personal brand and reputation. Engaging in meaningful conversations, sharing insights, and providing value to others not only helps build credibility but also increases the likelihood of being recognized as an expert or thought leader in one's field.

6. Opening Doors for Collaboration.

Networking fosters collaboration by connecting people with complementary skills and shared interests. Collaborative projects and partnerships can lead to innovative solutions, increased efficiency, and expanded business opportunities. By leveraging the diverse strengths and expertise within a network, you can achieve more significant outcomes and create synergistic relationships that benefit all parties involved.

7. Long-Term Career Development.

Networking plays a vital role in long-term career development. Building and maintaining a strong network ensures a continuous flow of information, support, and opportunities throughout your professional journey. As careers evolve, networking helps individuals adapt to changing circumstances, explore new paths, and connect with mentors or sponsors who can offer guidance and support during critical transitions.

Networking has become an indispensable tool for success in the business world. From creating opportunities and facilitating knowledge sharing to building supportive communities and enhancing visibility, the benefits of networking are vast. By actively engaging in networking activities, you can expand your professional horizons, gain access to valuable resources, and accelerate your growth and development. As the saying goes, "It's not just what you know, but who you know." Networking empowers you to cultivate meaningful relationships, open doors to new possibilities, and navigate the dynamic landscape of the business world with confidence and purpose.

Why networking is important to your success.

Experts agree that the most connected people are often the most successful. When you invest in your relationships — professional and personal — it can pay you back in dividends throughout the course of your career. Networking is essential since it will help you develop and improve your skill set, stay on top of the latest trends in your industry, keep a pulse on the job market, meet prospective mentors, partners, and clients, and gain access to the necessary resources that will foster your career development.

The importance of networking for career development.

Career development is the lifelong evolution of your career. It's influenced by a number of things that include the jobs you hold, the experiences you gain in and out of the office, the growth and success you achieve at each stage of your career, the formal and informal education and training you receive, and the feedback you're provided with along the way.

Ideally, organizations would place more emphasis on employee development in the workplace. However, the reality is that we live in what Carter Cast, author of the book, "The Right (and Wrong) Stuff: How Brilliant Careers Are Made," refers to as "the era of do-it-yourself career development."

Cast explains that in today's workforce, the burden is on you to take control of your career development. Hence the importance of networking for career development: As you network with people at your company, in your industry, and even outside your field of interest, you'll uncover opportunities to connect with different types of mentors and advisors, increase your visibility with senior management, further develop your areas of expertise, and improve your soft skills.

The importance of networking in the job search.

It goes without saying that networking is incredibly important during a job search. Your chances of landing the job increase tenfold with the right employee referral. And, if you're forced or looking to make a career change, your professional network can support you by helping you find connections in the industry you are trying to break into or helping you find leads for jobs at specific companies.

Take the time to build meaningful relationships with those in your professional circle, so when the time comes to search for work, you can tap into those valuable connections for referrals, insights into job leads, and other valuable information.

Statistics show that the majority of successful job searches are completed when the employee discovers a job through a networking contact. In fact, studies have found you're 10 times more likely to land a job when you know someone at the company.

Networking is essential for people looking to advance in their careers. According to HubSpot, networking accounts for 85% of job placements. According to CNBC, 70% of jobs are never publicly advertised.

These positions are either listed internally or developed particularly for candidates met through networking by recruiters. According to LinkedIn, 70% of professionals hired in the last few years had a connection at their firm, and 80% of professionals believe networking is critical to their professional success.

Though it's possible to acquire a job by sending your CV randomly to job boards and advertisements, these data clearly suggest that networking is the greatest method to building a successful career and sustaining job satisfaction.

How To Network Statistics

Thanks to social media sites like LinkedIn, online networking has taken over the business sector in the last decade as a tool for even larger networking opportunities.

LinkedIn was created expressly for those who want to network but can't always do so in person. Since then, millions of professionals have found success through online networking networks such as LinkedIn.

According to a LinkedIn research conducted in 2017, 35% of participants stated that a casual interaction via LinkedIn Messaging lead to a new opportunity. These opportunities may include employment or career changes, sales leads, or business transactions.

In fact, 25% of participants stated LinkedIn assisted them in forming a new business partnership. Furthermore, 61% of respondents believe that regular online connection with their network can lead to potential career prospects.

The following were the top advantages of social media and online networking:

- Saves time (92%)
- Saves money (88%)
- More flexibility in location and timing (76%)
- Allows the participant to multitask (64%)
- Increases productivity (55%)
- Ability to archive sessions (49%)
- Less peer pressure (16%)

In-Person Meetings.

COVID was a test for anyone who enjoys face-to-face networking. However, prior to the pandemic, in-person networking was crucial. According to HubSpot, virtually all professionals believe that face-to-face interactions are essential for maintaining long-term business ties.

According to a Forbes analysis, the top benefits of in-person encounters over technology-based networking are as follows. The following were the top advantages:

- Building stronger, more meaningful business relationships (85%)

- Better ability to read body language and facial expressions (77%)
- Ability to bond with co-workers/clients and more social interaction (75%)
- Allows for more complex strategic thinking (49%)
- Better environment for tough, timely decision-making (44%)
- Less opportunity for unnecessary distractions (40%)
- Leads to higher-quality decision-making (39%)
- Easier to focus (38%)
- Fewer disruptions and delays (23%)

As life gets back to normal, more and more people are bound to return to in-person networking due to its success in building business relationships.

Challenges of Networking

Insufficient Time

The main reason networking is difficult is that professionals do not always have the time to maintain their network. According to a LinkedIn survey, 49% of respondents indicated they didn't have enough time to network. According to HubSpot, approximately 41% of networkers would like to network more frequently but lack the time.

COVID PRE and POST.

It's difficult to talk about networking without mentioning the elephant in the room. Prior to 2020, many networkers would go to in-person gatherings to meet new clients and build business contacts.

However, COVID forced many people out of work and prevented professionals from interacting in person in a safe environment. The Pandemic also reduced the number of open positions. Many folks who have been laid off in the last two years are still looking.

The stigma attached to laid-off professionals prevented many from resuming their careers. Those laid off are frequently ashamed and less inclined to seek assistance from their network.

According to LinkedIn, only approximately 42% of professionals have sought out to existing contacts for job prospects since the pandemic began, and just 39% have requested people in their networks for introductions. Furthermore, just 35% of respondents have made their own introductions to new contacts.

Though the covid years have been difficult for business, the job market, and networking, there are signs that things are beginning to improve. Hopefully, things will return to normal shortly, and people will be able to network in person again safely.

Determine which networking style works best for you.

When it comes to networking, there is no "one size fits all" solution. Different people achieve success through various networking strategies. The idea is to experiment with several networking tactics to find out which one works best for you. For example, if you're an introvert, you might prefer to network one-on-one over coffee or attend more private events with fewer guests. Consider where you may go to meet the perfect people who can assist you in achieving your current career-development goals once you've identified your ideal networking approach.

Make a strategy.

While you don't have to know exactly what you want to achieve out of each networking event, it's crucial to walk in with a plan. For example, you might go to an event with the intention of meeting three new individuals in your business or gaining one new insight to share with your coworkers.

Following up.

Although it is a simple activity, many professionals overlook this essential stage in the networking process. The time you spent speaking with someone new will not aid your job advancement if you do not follow up. While you don't need to instantly send a long, meaningful message after meeting someone new, you should submit a LinkedIn connection request with a tailored note as soon as possible. When you have something valuable to contribute or a specific reason to reach out, save the meaningful message.

Spread the word.

Before you ask for support, look for ways to add value to individuals in your network. The more you invest in your relationships, the more you'll understand about your new contacts and the easier it will be to offer — and receive — support. Your value isn't confined to the office; it could range from a hotel recommendation to an introduction to someone in your personal network.

Final Thoughts On Networking.

Networking is essential in business and the job market. Most people get jobs through networking, and many sales and business leads are generated as a result of networking.

Despite these advantages, according to HubSpot, one out of every four professionals does not network at all. If you're one of these professionals, maybe this section has clarified why networking is so important for your job search and career.

CHAPTER TWENTY-TWO
The Inevitability of Change

The statement "nothing lasts forever" is often regarded as a reflection of the impermanence of things in life. While there are certain things that do not last forever, such as material possessions, relationships, and even life itself, it's important to note that some things can have lasting effects or endure for significant periods of time.

In the natural world, stars eventually exhaust their fuel and die, and even celestial bodies like planets and galaxies will undergo changes over time. Similarly, human life is finite, and we all experience changes and transitions throughout our lifetimes.

It's also important to remember that change and impermanence can bring new opportunities and growth. The transient nature of things allows for fresh experiences, learning, and the possibility of creating something new.

So while it's true that nothing lasts forever in its exact form, the impact, essence, or consequences of many things can endure beyond their individual existence.

Coping with failure and being forced to reinvent yourself and or your career can be a challenging and emotional experience, but it's an essential part of life and personal growth.

As stated in some of the earlier chapters, allow yourself to feel the disappointment, frustration, or sadness that accompanies failure. It's normal to experience a range of emotions, and acknowledging them is an important step in the healing process. Look for the lessons and opportunities for growth in the failure. Embrace the opportunity to learn and improve for future endeavors. Be kind and understanding to yourself. Remember that everyone fails at some point, and it does not define your worth or abilities. Treat yourself with the same compassion and understanding you would offer a friend in a similar situation.

Instead of viewing failure as an endpoint, see it as a stepping stone on your journey. Many successful individuals have experienced failures before achieving their goals. Embrace failure as an opportunity to build resilience and develop new strategies.

I have always used failure as motivation to set new goals or refine existing ones. I took the lessons learned and applied them to create a more effective plan of action.

Take care of your physical, emotional, and mental well-being. Engage in activities that bring you joy, relaxation, and rejuvenation. This can include exercise, hobbies, spending time with loved ones, or engaging in mindfulness and self-reflection practices.

Remember, failure is not the end. It's an opportunity for growth, resilience, and self-discovery. Embrace it as a natural part of life's journey and keep moving forward.

The statement "anything worth doing is difficult" is often used to emphasize the value and significance of pursuing challenging new endeavors. While it's true that many worthwhile pursuits require effort, dedication, and perseverance, it's important to note that not all valuable endeavors are necessarily difficult in the same way. Engaging in activities that push you out of your comfort zone and require effort lead to personal growth, self-discovery, and a sense of accomplishment. Overcoming challenges can build resilience, develop new skills, and expand your capabilities.

Often, endeavors that make a significant impact or contribute to the greater good require substantial effort. Whether it's starting a business, making a career change, or working towards a social cause, the challenges faced along the way can be an indication of the importance and potential impact of the work.

Becoming proficient in a new field or learning a new skill often requires dedication, practice, and perseverance. The journey toward mastery can be challenging, but it can also provide a deep sense of satisfaction and fulfillment.

However, it's worth noting that not all worthwhile pursuits are necessarily difficult in the traditional sense. Some endeavors may be more aligned with an individual's natural talents or passions, making them feel less arduous or demanding. Additionally, what one person finds difficult, another person may find relatively easier based on their unique strengths and experiences. Ultimately, the value of an endeavor should not solely be measured by its level of difficulty. It's important to consider factors such as personal interest, alignment with values, potential impact, and overall fulfillment when determining what is worth pursuing.

Final Thoughts

When facing a massive challenge, it can be helpful to break it down into smaller, more manageable steps or goals. By focusing on one step at a time, you can make progress and build momentum, gradually moving closer to your ultimate objective.

As I stated earlier, don't hesitate to reach out to others for support and guidance. Surround yourself with a network of friends, family, mentors, or professionals who can offer encouragement, advice, and assistance. Sometimes, having someone by your side can provide the motivation and perspective needed to tackle the seemingly impossible.

Also, don't forget to create a well-thought-out plan or strategy that outlines the necessary actions and resources needed to overcome the odds. Break down the challenge into specific tasks, set achievable milestones, and track your progress along the way. A clear plan can provide structure, direction, and a sense of control amidst adversity. Developing resilience is crucial when facing insurmountable odds. Embrace a positive mindset, believe in your abilities, and maintain a "never give up" attitude. Accept that setbacks and obstacles are a natural part of the journey, and view them as opportunities to learn, grow, and adapt.

Seek out stories of individuals who have overcome seemingly impossible odds. Read biographies, watch documentaries, or connect with people who have faced similar challenges. Learning about other people's journeys and successes can provide inspiration, instill hope, and demonstrate that extraordinary feats can be achieved.

Flexibility and adaptability are key when dealing with daunting odds. Sometimes, the initial plan may need adjustments along the way. Stay open to alternative approaches, be willing to learn and pivot when necessary, and consider different perspectives or solutions that may lead to breakthroughs.

Recognize and celebrate the progress you make, no matter how small it may seem. Each step forward is a testament to your resilience and determination. Acknowledging your achievements along the way can provide the motivation and confidence to continue pushing forward.

Remember, even when facing seemingly insurmountable odds, the human spirit has an incredible capacity to overcome challenges. By breaking them down, seeking support, planning strategically, cultivating resilience, finding inspiration, staying adaptable, and celebrating progress, you can increase your chances of getting beyond those obstacles and achieving what may have seemed impossible.

Stay focused. Good luck.

www.ingramcontent.com/pod-product-compliance
Lightning Source LLC
Chambersburg PA
CBHW070011300526
45794CB00001B/277